D0431042

BANKS TO SANDBERG TO GRACE

Five Decades of Love and Frustration with the Chicago Cubs

COMPILED BY
CARRIE MUSKAT

FOREWORD BY BOB VERDI

Contemporary Books

Chicago New York San Francisco Lisbon London Madrid Mexico City
Milan New Delhi San Juan Seoul Singapore Sydney Toronto

Library of Congress Cataloging-in-Publication Data

Banks to Sandberg to Grace : five decades of love and frustration with the Chicago Cubs / compiled by Carrie Muskat.
      p.   cm.
Includes index.
ISBN 0-8092-9712-4 (hardcover)
ISBN 0-07-138556-8 (paperback)
     1. Chicago Cubs (Baseball team)—Interviews.   I. Title: Five decades of love and frustration with the Chicago Cubs.   II. Muskat, Carrie.

GV875.C6 B35   2001
796.357'64'0977311—dc21   00-60315

Contemporary Books

A Division of The **McGraw·Hill** Companies

1 2 3 4 5 6 7 8 9 0   AGM/AGM   0 9 8 7 6 5 4 3 2

ISBN 0-8092-9712-4 (hardcover)
ISBN 0-07-138556-8 (paperback)

This book was set in Bembo
Printed and bound by Quebecor Martinsburg

Cover and interior design by Nick Panos
Front jacket photograph by Stephen Green
Interior illustrations copyright © Keith Witmer
Grateful acknowledgment is made to Stephen Green and the Baseball Hall of Fame Library

McGraw-Hill books are available at special quantity discounts to use as premiums and sales promotions, or for use in corporate training programs. For more information, please write to the Director of Special Sales, Professional Publishing, McGraw-Hill, Two Penn Plaza, New York, NY 10121-2298. Or contact your local bookstore.

This book is printed on acid-free paper.

To my hero, Alan

CONTENTS

1960s

1970s

1980s

1990s

FOREWORD

There are two ways a writer can go about this business of reporting sports. He or she can do the scores or highlights routine, and toss in a few quotations for filler. Or, one can cultivate this fertile field, unearthing insights and nuggets of news that cannot be found elsewhere and thus require extra effort. We all admire athletes who "give 100 percent" every game; I feel the same about journalists who do likewise.

Carrie Muskat belongs in the latter category, which is one reason why I was so excited to hear about her latest work, *Banks to Sandberg to Grace*. Talk about a fertile field: the Cubs have been making baseball fans laugh and cry for decades. They have had only 13 winning seasons since their last World Series appearance in 1945, but they're forever piquing our interest—whether it's Jose Cardenal missing part of spring training because his eyelids were stuck together or relief pitchers lighting fires they were supposed to put out.

I remember watching a game when the Cubs lost 22–0 to Pittsburgh, and the Cubs were lucky to get nothing. There was another time when I was out for a day and came home and someone said the Cubs scored 26 runs in Denver. My first question was, "Did they win?"

I can think of no other journalist better qualified to tell us all about it than Carrie. Almost without fail, in her daily dispatches, she reports what you want to know about a game, or a person, or a situation. Moreover, she will find something that no other journalist has.

"I didn't know that." I can't tell you how many times I've whispered that to myself after reading one of Carrie's stories, whether she's covering just another ballgame on a Tuesday afternoon in August or writing an extended feature from some distant dateline. I've been in the racket for a long time, so I respect her work ethic and her instincts. There's a lot of stuff teams and players don't want reporters to write, but Carrie has that knack of pursuing, whether it's a fact she's after or an explanation. It's not easy, because the competition is fierce, but Carrie hits a lot of home runs.

I'm confident you'll feel that way about this book. She has interviewed numerous Cubs, from then and now, and pulled it all together. She's not afraid to let other people talk, and that is a gift with which some reporters are not blessed. We all ask questions, but how many of us are good listeners? Carrie has seen a lot, and what she hasn't seen of the Cubs during the last 50 or so lean years, she's studied and researched. She also realizes that sports are part of the entertainment industry and writes accordingly.

We read about sports because they are diversions, and while she takes her job seriously, Carrie has just the right light touch. There is no substitute for being there, and I've seen it in person. She arrives at the ballpark early and leaves late. I never particularly enjoyed working against her, but I know you'll enjoy this book as much as I did. If anyone can make sense of the Cubs, it's Carrie Muskat.

Bob Verdi

INTRODUCTION

My favorite time at Wrigley Field is early, before any fans are allowed in. It's too soon for batting practice. The grounds crew has finished raking the infield dirt smooth. The batting cage and screens are in place. Wrigley is quiet, respectful, pure. And there is anticipation in the air, because you never know what is going to happen that day. Andre Dawson could hit three home runs in consecutive at bats. The lights could come on. Kerry Wood could strike out 20.

That's why I like my job as a baseball writer. And that's part of the reason Cub fans keep coming back.

The Cubs are a franchise that has often been comically incompetent, home to sometimes-endearing characters and not a few truly great players, and tinged by racism and upper-management whimsy. A franchise that has provided brief moments of intense joy in an aura that includes a wonderful ballpark and, especially recently, fans who keep on coming despite everything. No other franchise in sports has all that.

Every time Lou Brock's name is mentioned, Cub fans cringe. How could Leon Durham miss that ground ball in '84? Why isn't Greg Maddux still a Cub? Why didn't the Cubs win the World Series in '45? How did Ernie Banks really feel about Leo Durocher? What happened in '69? What was Lee Elia thinking when he blasted Cub fans? If Hank Sauer ran a foot race with Ralph Kiner, would anybody win?

Need answers? Read on. You will be surprised.

This is a story of the Chicago Cubs—more than a half century of failure—in the words of the very people who were so much a part of it. I interviewed more than 60 players, coaches, managers, and others, and let them talk. What you're about to read is what they said, how they said it.

All of the interviews were done exclusively for this book with the exception of Sammy Sosa's. He did not want to take part because, as he put it, "I have my own book." The material in his chapter is from a one-on-one interview conducted in August 1999.

Many thanks to all who shared their stories. Thanks also to Arlene Gill, Rebecca Polihronis, and John McDonough of the Cubs for helping me find some of these guys; to Sharon Pannozzo and Chuck Wasserstrom for always being there; to Steve Green and Steven Schwab—they know why; and to Bob Verdi for his kind words.

And, to my husband, Alan Solomon, a baseball fan, former Wrigley vendor, and still an occasional (right field) bleacher bum, thanks for your inspiration, insight, and editing skills. I couldn't have done this without you.

Phil Cavarretta

A native Chicagoan, Phil Cavarretta was signed out of Lane Tech High School and played 20 years for the Cubs. His signing bonus? "I signed for a bag of peanuts," he said. The Cubs paid him $125 a month and he sent half of that home to his Italian immigrant parents. At the age of 18, he homered in his first major league at bat, but never became a serious power hitter. Nicknamed Phillibuck, his best year was 1945 when he batted a league-leading .355 and won Most Valuable Player honors. He paced the Cubs in their seven-game World Series loss to Detroit, batting .423. Cavarretta was promoted to manager in 1951, replacing Frankie Frisch, but his honesty got the best of him. He was fired in spring training 1954 when he criticized the Cubs' chances. And today? "I sit there and second-guess the hell out of them," he says.

I came to the Cubs right out of high school. I had just two and a half months' experience in Class A and I was called up. I was blessed with ability. The good Lord says he'll put you on earth to become a professional baseball player, and he says it's going to be up to you to play hard and be successful. That's the truth. That's why I always gave 110 percent.

My parents were from Italy. They could hardly speak English. It was during the depression in '35 and I made the Cubs, and my parents were happy about it but they didn't understand baseball. When I was going to school, I played softball. I played in the yard and was sliding around and getting all dirty and my pants all torn up. I'd come home and my dad would look at me and I'm all filthy. He'd look at me and he'd say, "Philly, where you been?"

I said, "Dad, I've been out in the schoolyard playing baseball with my friends."

He said, "Baseball? What the hell is baseball? Baseball, you forget. You go to school, learn your books."

My dad became a good baseball fan and he came out to Wrigley Field with my mom. He'd go into the office before the game, and he'd say, "My son, Phillip, he win the ballgame for the Cubs today, OK?"

My dad had a beautiful curly mustache and a big one. He had blue eyes like Frank Sinatra. He was a good-looking guy. He'd always sit there and curl the ends of his mustache up.

I played my first game and it was early in April. It was cold and there were snowflakes. I had a pretty good night. The first time up, I hit a home run. I hit for the cycle in the minors. The Cubs sent me a telegram that said, "Report to Reading, Pennsylvania," and at that time it was the Boston Red Sox farm team. I told Mr. [Clarence "Pants"] Rowland, "That's not one of our affiliates." I had a pretty good year, hit .318, .320. Being just an 18-year-old kid, I was homesick. The last game, I'm packing my bag and I get another telegram that said, "Report to the Cubs." I wanted to go home but I was happy.

I know a lot of people weren't too fond of Mr. Wrigley, but to me, he was very, very good. He was very quiet and very reserved. He looked like he was always sitting and thinking, "What move am I going to make with my gum company?" If he took a liking to you, he was your friend. He enjoyed us. He wouldn't come out and yell and all that stuff. Mrs. Wrigley, she was just the opposite. She'd come out there every day and sit in her box seat and she'd root for the Cubbies. She had a ball.

Mr. Wrigley was generous. During those days, the majority of the owners wouldn't put their money out because they weren't drawing two, three million people. The money wasn't there. Mr. Wrigley, he took care of us pretty good. He'd give us a bonus every once in a while. He was his own man. That's it. I enjoyed him.

Favorite moment? My first game. That was the highest, most thrilling moment I ever had. I came up to the Cubs, and I picked them up in Boston and from Boston we came home to Wrigley Field. I played my first game September 25, 1934. I was just 18 years old. We were playing Cincinnati. The pitcher was Whitey Wistert—when you do something good against a guy, you remember. He had two brothers who went to the University of Michigan. Whitey was a pretty good pitcher. He, too, was a rookie. It was 0–0 going into the seventh inning. I wasn't a home run hitter. I was like Mark Grace. I hit a home run and we won 1–0. Charlie Root was our pitcher. When I became manager, he was my pitching coach, a beautiful guy and a good pitcher.

Now a year later, September 25, 1935, we're in St. Louis and we're battling the Cardinals for the pennant. This is the old Gashouse Gang. I'm talking about a good club. Dizzy Dean, Leo Durocher, Joe Medwick, Pepper Martin—they had a pretty good club. It's 0–0, same thing. We had a five-game series there. If we win the first game, we're tied for the pennant. Lon Warneke was our pitcher. Same inning, seventh inning. I hit a home run against Paul Dean. And the score was 1–0.

We clinched the pennant the next day. I think it was Charlie Root who beat Dizzy Dean. Dizzy Dean was one of my favorite guys after he went to broadcasting. He was a real funny guy. Great sense of humor.

The Cubs changed managers in the middle of the '38 season. Charlie Grimm was our manager. We were just playing average. We did have a pretty good team. We had all the players from the '35 team, which was a young, feisty bunch of guys. That team, most people don't know it—I think it's still a record. In the month of September, we won 21 games in a row. That was pretty good. I was only 18 years old and right out of high school, and I'm in a World Series. That was the '35 team. In '38, we had the same ballclub as '35, and we weren't playing too good. Maybe we were getting a little feisty like all people do. Maybe we thought we were king of the hill. They named Gabby Hartnett, who was our catcher, the manager. Charlie, he was so good to me, he was a jolly guy all the time. He treated everybody like his own son. That was great, but I guess that kind of wore out. They hired Gabby, who was a great player and a Hall of Famer. He was tough and the opposite. That shook us up.

That's the year Gabby hit the home run in the dark and, believe me, it was dark. No lights and we had two men out, and Mace Brown was pitching for the Pirates and a super relief pitcher. He got the first two men out and he got two strikes on Gabby and a bell must have rang in his brain. He's throwing all fastballs. He must have figured Gabby couldn't see too good. He decided to throw a slider. A slider doesn't have too much velocity, and he did Gabby a favor. He did us all a favor. The ball didn't look like it was going to get high enough. I guess the good Lord said, "Let me get this thing up a few inches." I'm a strong believer in the man up above.

We went on to win the pennant in '38, and we faced a team that was unbelievable. The '38 Yankees were pretty damn good. Coming back from New York, Gabby wasn't too happy about it. We were in one of the compartments there on the train. We were allowed to play poker then. We had a few beers in there, and he found out we were in there. He knocked on the door and we opened it up; we knew who it was. He was pretty feisty. He had had a few beers, too. He read us the riot act. "You goddamn so and so, how can you go in there and celebrate? You lost four in a row." He said, "Let me tell you another thing—half you guys won't be here next year." Believe me, half of those guys were gone. It hurt our club. We finished fourth in '39.

Gabby was a great guy, but he was a tough loser. That's why they called him Gabby—he was always yakking, pep talks. I'd like to see more of that today.

In the middle of the '45 season, the war was over and a lot of the good players came back, and things got a little tough then. We had a good ballclub. We had Andy Pafko, and Bill Nicholson, and myself, and Claude Passeau, and Stan Hack. That was a pretty good club, war year or no war year. Again, Charlie Grimm was our manager. We just kind of stayed together so to speak. We won the pennant and again we got in the World Series. I was in three World Series and I haven't won one yet.

Detroit, they had a good club. Once the war was over, Virgil Trucks came out, and Hank Greenberg and Hal Newhouser. Those were two pretty good clubs. Deep down in my heart, I felt we should've won it. It went down to seven games. What happened was, in the sixth game, Hank Borowy was pitching—and I don't mean to be second-guessing Charlie, but Hank Borowy wasn't a big guy and he wasn't too strong. We got him from the Yankees in a trade, and they paid $100,000 for him. The key to Hank Borowy was he could beat most of the clubs. The team he could beat and do an outstanding job against was the Cardinals. That was the team we had to beat. Without Borowy, we wouldn't have won the pennant.

Hank pitched the second game and won, and he started another game and didn't do too good. That's two games in six days. That's a lot. He wasn't that strong, bodywise. That could happen to anybody. We came down to play the seventh game at Wrigley Field, and Charlie decides to start him, and this was his third time. The guy was out of gas and he showed it the first inning. They bombed him for four runs, and there went the Series. You do your best to win. We heard he was going to start Borowy and said,

7

"Oh, my God." We had Hank Wyse. Claude Passeau—he was hit by a line drive. If he'd been sound, he would've started. In my opinion, and this sounds like a Cub, Passeau would've beat them.

In '51, I was a player and we were playing the Phillies and we had all the white shirts out there in the [center field] bleachers. That's when they had the Whiz Kids, Curt Simmons and Robin Roberts, good club. It was the fifth or sixth inning. Curt Simmons was the type of pitcher who was up on top, straight overhand. The ball was tough to pick up, let alone try to hit it against that background. This is the second game of a doubleheader. White ball, white background. The pitcher was in the sun, the hitter in the shade. He throws a ball and I try to pick it up on release point so to speak. When he let it go, I saw it but when it got in the background I lost it. Then it was right in my eyes. So I threw up my right arm, like a boxer would do for protection. It hit me in my right arm and fractured it. If I didn't do that, I wouldn't be talking to you today.

When I became manager in '52, I went up to Wid Matthews, who was the general manager at that time. I said, "We've got to do something about that background."

He said, "What are you talking about?" and I told him the story I just told you. He said, "Let me think about it. I don't know what we can do."

I said, "What do you mean, you don't know what you can do?"

He said, "That means we'd have to rope off 1,200 seats."

I said, "So what? Is it more important to lose those seats or lose Hank Sauer or Ralph Kiner or somebody else?"

They put boards across there and painted it green. Now when I see it, it looks pretty good. I'd like to hit against that.

I went back to Chicago and I was sitting in a box seat, and this old lady comes up to me and says what a big fan she was of mine. She gave me a hug and a kiss. She said she's been coming out to

Wrigley Field for 35 years. She gave me another kiss and left. Five minutes later, someone else gives me a tap on the shoulder and it's a nun. She said, "I just wanted to come over and say hello to you, Phil." Cub fans, they love you, win, lose, or draw. They had a Cavarretta fan club in '44, '45. They'd bring me cookies.

Andy Pafko

The Cubs in the World Series? Andy Pafko remembers. He starred at center field for the Cubs in 1945 when they reached the Series against Detroit—which the Cubs lost in seven games. Pafko doesn't recall much hoopla about the Series. Named to the Cubs' All-Century team, he is also known for a fluke play a few years later. On April 30, 1949, against St. Louis, Pafko made what he thought was a game-ending catch of Rocky Nelson's fly ball. Cubs win, right? But umpire Al Barlick ruled Pafko had trapped the ball and, as the two argued, Nelson dashed for a two-run inside-the-park homer. The Cardinals won 4–3. Pafko calls it the "home run in a glove."

When we got into the World Series, I talked to a number of people who said they couldn't get a ticket. It was exciting but I can't remember that much excitement. In those days, there wasn't TV and it wasn't all over the country, it was more local. It should've been exciting, but I don't remember.

Oh, the "home run in a glove." We had a one-run lead going into the ninth inning. The game was played at Wrigley Field. Enos Slaughter, he got on base. He was on first base and there are two out. Rocky Nelson, I don't know if he was playing or pinch-hitting. He hit one of those little short Texas League fly balls. I dove for the ball for the third out. I know definitely that I caught the ball. Little did I know Al Barlick, who was umpiring, said I trapped the ball. I didn't know that. I started walking off the field.

Peanuts Lowrey said, "Throw the ball." I just ignored all the runners completely. I was over arguing with Al Barlick. Peanuts Lowrey said, "Throw the ball, throw the ball!"

In the meantime, both runners are 20 feet from home plate, and I threw it and hit someone in the back. Both runs scored and we lost that game by one run. To me, it was the saddest moment of my life. That particular play lost us the ballgame. I was really upset. But I caught the ball. In those days, there was no TV. There was no replay. But I know definitely I caught the ball in the pocket of my glove. If I'd caught it in the webbing, I would've scooped it up in the grass.

I retired from baseball and Al Barlick, who was one of the great umpires in the game, retired about seven or eight years later. We had an old-timers game in Washington, D.C. I walk into the hotel lobby and there's Barlick. He doesn't say, "Andy, how are you? Nice to see you." The first thing he tells me is, "Hey, Andy, you still did not catch that ball." He still denies it. I definitely caught the ball. To my dying day, I'll say I caught the ball.

Charlie Grimm was a wonderful man. He was like a father to me. I played for him twice, here in Chicago and in Milwaukee. He was a wonderful guy, easy guy to play for. He enjoyed the game. He was happy-go-lucky. He was manager and he also coached third base. He put on a show when the guys were sliding into third, he'd go down on his stomach. When guys were trying to score, he'd run along the third base line. I would describe him as a baseball character. He had a lot of fun. Baseball is a serious game. He enjoyed it. When the game was over and we'd lost a close game, he'd go around and slap people on the back and say, "Tomorrow is another day. We'll get 'em tomorrow." Jolly Cholly, that was an appropriate name. After the World Series was over, even though we lost, he said, "Boy, this is wonderful, Andy. What a game."

People say, "What's different in baseball?" We always traveled strictly by train. We only had eight teams in each league—now there are 30 major league clubs. We didn't play on artificial turf. There was no night baseball either. Of course, the biggest change is the salaries. That's the biggest change. There was no minimum when I played. We had no TV revenue. It was strictly from attendance. I had some pretty good years with the Cubs and I had a heck of a time getting a raise. They said we didn't draw no fans. There was no money coming in. The most money I made was $35,000 and that was in 1950. That's tip money today. In those days, it was big money. I was a major league player. That was what I was striving for. I was glad to have a job.

Another big change, all the players have agents. I had no agent. I was my own agent. I had to go to Wrigley Field and talk on my behalf. One year I had to go downtown to see Mr. Wrigley. When I played, it was strictly a sport. Now, it's big business, plain and simple. It's still a great game, it's baseball, but the game has changed. I don't know how people can afford to go to baseball games. They say it costs a couple with two children $150 and even more by the time you buy tickets and parking and food. I feel sorry for the fans.

When I played, the first $100,000 ballplayers were Ted Williams, Stan Musial, and Joe DiMaggio. Can you imagine what those guys would be making if they were playing today? People say, "Don't you wish you were playing today?"

I say, "Yes and no. Yes for the salary. But no, because when I played, it was real baseball."

Maybe one of these days it will go the other way for the Cubs. Hopefully, hopefully. People say, "What do you think of the Cubs' chances?" I always tell them, "Number one, you've got to have the pitching." It's like when I was in the World Series with the Dodgers. And I tell people you have to be strong through the middle. Catching, pitching, middle infield. We had Duke Snider and [Roy] Campanella and [Pee Wee] Reese and [Jackie] Robinson.

If the Cubs get any decent pitching, they'll have a chance in their division. It's like they're jinxed or something. It's like that billy goat thing, although I think that's a bunch of talk. You've got to have the personnel.

Hank Wyse

Hank Wyse usually kept his 1945 World Series ring locked up at home. It was a reminder of a disappointing experience. Manager Charlie Grimm opted to start Hank Borowy in Game 7 against Detroit while Wyse, a 22-game winner that year, made only one start. Borowy threw a six-hit shutout in Game 1, went five innings in Game 5, pitched four innings of relief in Game 6, and then started Game 7. He ran out of gas, and the Cubs lost the finale, 9–3, and the Series. Wyse could only watch and wonder, "What if?" He died in October 2000.

We didn't lose that World Series. Charlie Grimm did. Because he pitched Borowy all the time. He pitched the one he thought would win. I can't imagine me winning 22 and pitching one game in a seven-game series. Sure, I was disappointed. A lot of other players were disappointed, too.

The biggest surprise during the season was pitching on two or three days' rest. Charlie had me in front of all the coaches and he said, "You think you could pitch on two days' rest?"

I said, "What would happen if I hurt my arm?"

He said, "Mr. Wrigley will take care of you for the rest of your life."

He didn't, but I didn't ask him either. He might have given me a package of gum. I wish I was playing now. I'd be making more money.

Charlie Grimm didn't pitch the players right. He might have played most of them right, but he didn't pitch them right. He liked to pitch me to death. Two days' rest, three days' rest. I relieved on the side. I think that's how come we won the pennant, all the pitching I did.

I should've started more than one game in a seven-game series. He never explained it. He was a pretty good clown, though. He kidded around and pulled a lot of things. He was real funny. He did it for the crowd. He'd let line drives go right past him and he'd stick his hand out and catch it and throw the ball back to the pitcher. Then he'd put his hand in his hip pocket because it hurt. He went over one time to Roy Hughes, who hit a triple. It was muddy that day. Charlie had his left hand on Roy's shoulder and he brushed his pants off down to the bottom and then brushed his hips off, and Hughes said, "That's enough." He hit another triple in the same game. Charlie did it again and he got mud all over his hand and then he wiped Hughes' back with his muddy hand. He was Jolly Cholly. He was always doing something funny and laughing.

I've got a bat that was Rogers Hornsby's and I got my name on it. I'm going to keep that and give it to some of the kids when I pass away. I never used that bat but I did use his bat [a Hornsby model] in games. A lot of guys have tried to buy it from me.

I was an electrician for 40 years. I did that while I was playing. I made more money being an electrician than playing ball. I welded, too, and that was a bonus. I got extra hours, overtime. Sometimes I made pretty good money.

I miss it a lot. I had a lot of fun playing ball. Yeah, I remember some of the games real well. Some I can hardly remember, but I guess that's when I had a bad day.

Claude Passeau

Claude Passeau was most proud of his innings pitched. He ignored bone chips in his right elbow in 1945 to go 17–9 and help the Cubs reach the World Series. His postgame regimen? "I took a bath and went home," he said. Passeau threw a one-hit, 3–0 shutout in the third game of the Series against Detroit and had a 5–1 lead in the seventh inning of Game 6 when he was hit on the right ring finger by a line drive off Jimmy Outlaw's bat. Passeau had to leave the game, but the Cubs held on for an 12-inning win. Hank Borowy finished up Game 6 and had nothing for the decisive seventh game, which the Tigers won 9–3. Passeau after 1947 and served as sheriff in his native Lucedale, Mis eight years. Fishing now takes up most of his time.

I just took my eyes off the ball and it hit me on the ring my right hand. It swole up and I couldn't hold the ball. If it han't been for that sixth game, I think we would've won. I tried to pitch like that, and it was just like pitching batting practice. I still believe we would've won the Series.

The World Series was exciting, but like my wife says, "You never got excited about anything." I never got excited. When we went to start the '45 Series, the skipper told me, "So-and-so is going to pitch the first game and so-and-so is going to pitch the second game and you're going to pitch the third game. I'm not going to tell any of the writers that you're going to pitch the third game."

My wife couldn't get a seat anywhere but behind a post and she sat with the gamblers. I said, "Don't tell anybody who you are." I believe it was Borowy in the first game and he was 5 to 5 and Wyse pitched the second game and he was 6 to 5 and when they made the announcement about me, the gamblers made me 8 to 5. The gamblers were on the third base side. They set the odds and that's the way they bet—it's going to be a strike, it's going to be a ball, it's going to be high. My wife said she saw more $100 bills that day than she ever heard of.

I never fooled with them. It was just a no-no as far as baseball players are concerned. I think Pete Rose is being cheated right now or has been ever since he stopped playing. He was a wonderful ballplayer, a good ballplayer. I just admire him that he played as hard as he did.

When I was traded to the Cubs, I called my wife and told her to pack up. I was in Boston. I told her, "I'll be home tomorrow and I want you to be packed up and we'll go the next day to the Cubs." About the second day after I got there, Ed Burns, the writer, wrote a column. The headline was, "What the Hell Do the Cubs Want with Passeau?" My wife was mad because they said such a thing. I didn't save it. I just laughed and threw it away.

A lot of the stars and some of the better players were in the service, and I figured the teams weren't as productive, I guess you could say. I tried to get a raise after the season, after we got through playing. They said, "You didn't win but 17." They gave me a little raise, like $2,000.

I went up and talked to Mr. Wrigley one time. I'd won 20 and I like to sign my contract before I go home and I went up to talk to him and we talked about boots and airplanes and everything else. And finally he says, "I know you didn't come up here to just talk." He was a businessman and a baseball man.

I said, "Mr. Wrigley, I won 20 and that ought to be worth $20,000 and I relieved some, and saved some, and pitched on four-day schedules for six, eight years, and never missed a turn, and was always in good shape."

He says, "Well, you lost seven."

I said, "Well, Mr. Wrigley, I don't count the ones I lose, just the ones I win."

The most money I ever made was $20,000 and that was after I'd won 20. Times have changed.

You went to the better restaurants, you'd get better meat like steak and what have you. It was fun while it lasted. I didn't do without anything. I wasn't too much of a nightlifer, I wasn't much of one at all. I was just a ballplayer.

When it came my day to pitch, I pitched. I had 189 complete games—one in the World Series. I guess I could have made a little more money, but I didn't hold out or do this or that. They treated me nice.

I don't ever remember missing but one start. I slid into second base and under the shortstop's knee and cracked a rib. I missed one turn. It was pretty sore. That put me out a week or 10 days.

When it was my turn to work, I went to work and no foolishness. I was listening to a talk show from San Diego after I quit playing ball and they were interviewing Clyde McCullough. They said, "Clyde, you caught for the Cubs."

Ol' Clyde said, "I did a good job of it, too."

They said, "You caught Passeau, didn't you?"

He said, "Yes, sir."

"Which was the best pitcher you ever caught?"

Clyde said, "Well, I don't want to say, but I'll tell you one thing about Passeau. When it was his day to pitch, he was a nice fellow until he got to that white line and then when he crossed that line he was the meanest fellow I ever knowed." I had to laugh at that.

I never hit anybody in the head. I hit one or two maybe in the back, but never hit anybody to hurt them. I played 16 years and I never had a man, a hitter, come out to the mound. I had one fellow from Brooklyn and he threw me a curveball and hit me right over the shoulder blade in the back. The score was 9–2 in the ninth inning, so I got mad at him and I threw my bat at him. If it had been 3–2, nothing would've been said. But 9–2, game in our favor in the ninth inning, you don't throw at somebody like that. You should remember that for the next time.

Ransom Jackson

"Handsome Ransom" Jackson was the Cubs' regular third baseman from 1950 to 1955, and although some players complain about day games wearing them down, he enjoyed them. It was as close to being a nine-to-five job and a regular lifestyle as a ballplayer could get. Jackson played for Frankie Frisch, Phil Cavarretta, and Stan Hack and was present when young Ernie Banks and Gene Baker arrived in 1953, the first African American players on the Cubs. Jackson says he doesn't recall a team meeting or special preparation. Banks and Baker just showed up and played. Jackson does remember some other details about playing in the '50s.

I remember—and this is probably true for anyone who has ever played for the Cubs—they love the hours. It's a daytime job. You go to work at 9:30 and get off at 4:30. It was a great place to play because of that.

Chicago fans were probably the best fans I was ever around. Back then, we drew only 6,000 or 7,000 a game—we were habitually a seventh- or eighth-place team. I think one year we came in fourth and everybody got a check for $200. The fans, you love the fans. I really enjoyed being around them. Of course, there were some . . . but the majority came out to see baseball and loved the Cubs win or lose.

I only see the Cubs on TV occasionally now. It's the same old thing. They don't win. I don't know why they don't win now. I played six years and we had some idiots up in the front office.

They would automatically trade for any ballplayer that Brooklyn was ready to get rid of.

In 1955, I was the only Cub to go to the All-Star Game. I hit 21 home runs and I was out for a month and a half with an infected hand, and I had to fight for a $1,500 raise. Today, they get these three-, four-, five-year contracts. Back then, one year was the most, and they had people in the wings who were waiting to take our place. Today, you've got guys sitting on the bench making a couple million dollars.

In all honesty, Phil [Cavarretta] wasn't the most brilliant manager in the world. We had some good guys and some idiots, too. Frankie Frisch, he was a great ballplayer but as a manager, he wasn't very good.

We used to train on Catalina Island. Somebody had the great idea to go out two weeks early, and they had wild goats out there on the island. They had the idea to go out and run on the goat trails to build up leg strength and get in shape. Well, after two weeks, everybody got shinsplints.

I'm not going to say I was a saint, but at least I went home at a reasonable hour. I was prone to stay out all night when things weren't going too good. I think there was one time when the season started and I was hitting every ball on the nose and wasn't getting any hits. I stayed out all night long and I started getting some hits after that.

It was the old-timers playing back in the '40s who did a lot of staying out late. Most of the younger guys were pretty conscientious. It's nice to go out occasionally; you can't go from a game to home. It was a different story if you had a family.

When I went to school at the University of Texas, I can't remember any blacks who played baseball or football. I never thought about it at the time. When I played a couple years in the minors [in '48 and '49] there were a few black players, and it never bothered me at all. I figured if a guy could play, he could play. I played side by side with Ernie [Banks] for three years. It was a great relationship. I never felt that because he was another color I shouldn't be playing with him.

They never said a word. There were blacks on every team by then. Just because we didn't have any, it was just a coincidence. Nobody said, "Hey, you white guys go over in the corner." Nobody said, "Hey, I'm not going to have my locker near Ernie or Gene."

All through college, I played lots of sports and it was always "Ransom." Nobody plays under your real name in baseball. I guess "Randy" started in baseball. I got up to the major leagues and some sportswriter said, "We'll throw another one on there and we'll make it 'Handsome Ransom.'" Now, when I go to card shows, they say, "Can you please sign it 'Handsome Ransom Jackson'?"

Hank Sauer

He was known as the Mayor of Wrigley Field. On the day he was interviewed, he proudly boasted that he had shot an 81. Not bad for an 82-year-old man. The big right-handed hitting outfielder didn't do too poorly on the playing field either. He won the 1952 National League Most Valuable Player Award, batting .270 with 37 home runs and 121 runs batted in. That season, the Cubs were 77–77 and finished fifth under manager Phil Cavarretta. In midseason, Sauer shifted from left field, where he was showered with packets of chewing tobacco, to right field to make room for Ralph Kiner. Frankie Baumholtz was in center. They weren't the fastest outfield, but they had a good time. Sauer died in August 2000, on a golf course near his northern California home.

As far as I'm concerned, I was one way. I wanted to win. There was no other way I could play. We had a good year that year [1952]—actually, it wasn't a good year. But I gave them 100 percent, and I did the best I could. Can I say that I carried that ballclub? No. There were so many good ballplayers on the ballclub who gave 100 percent, which is all you can do in the big leagues because you have to. If you don't, you won't last long.

I had a pretty good year in '52. The only thing I can say is I thank God I was picked [for the MVP]. I can't say nothing but the best about the other two guys, Robin Roberts and Joe Black. It was nice that I was picked ahead of them.

I went out there and the people in left field, they were such a sweet bunch. Every time we went out there, especially if I hit a home run, it rained chewing tobacco. I loved it. It kept me going, that chewing tobacco. The people in Chicago were absolutely super. I don't chew now, but I did then and I enjoyed it. The only thing it ever did for me was that it relaxed me. I enjoyed the people for one simple reason—they threw it down there and I picked it up and I enjoyed it.

I chewed when I played golf. When I had to quit, it killed me. It was fun. Why I say it was fun, I can't tell you the reason for it. It relaxed me, so it made me play better. I don't think it happened to me alone. It happened to a lot of ballplayers. Relax, and go out to the ballpark, and enjoy what you're doing.

There's one thing I always remember: I asked Phil, I said, "Phil, why don't you make me stay in left field? Those are my people out there, my great friends. Why would you switch me to right?"

He said, "Hank, I got to."

Neither one of us were speed merchants. That's why I went to right field. I'm not saying nothing bad about Ralph. He was a great guy, a great player. I had to go to right because I could run a little bit better than him, I could throw a little bit better than him, and Ralph was getting to the point where he was having some bad years, but there's not a nicer person in the world than Ralph Kiner. He was a good guy. We had a lot of fun together. I could outrun him. That's one thing that I could do.

Phil, he was a real good friend of mine. When he went from player to manager, we were still good friends. I gave him everything he wanted and everything I had. He was a wonderful person. Something tells me he doesn't get enough of what he deserves in Chicago. He was like a little kid when he first got there. He and I and Frankie ran around together until Phil became manager. Then we had to separate. Then we got divorced. We were the kind of guys who might have a beer or two after the game.

We didn't make any money playing. In five years, my biggest raise was when I got to be MVP in '52. I got up to $37,500. The other years, my greatest year, my best year, I got a $3,000 or $4,000 raise. That was 100 years ago. I think it was 100 years ago. All I can say is if it wasn't for baseball, I don't know what I would be doing. I would've been sweeping the streets, but I would've been the best street sweeper in Pennsylvania.

What I've never forgotten and I never will is I played for the greatest people in Chicago. As long as I've played in this game, they are the greatest people that ever lived. I don't think anybody could ever believe they could play in a greater town than Chicago. You give the people of Chicago 100 percent of your ability and they will love you. You hit .220, but you give 100 percent and they love you. You strike out two or three times, hit into a double play two or three times, but if you run out balls, you run hard to first, the little things they notice. That's how great the people of Chicago were. They were the kind of people who just knew. If you give them 100 percent, you'll never get booed. If you screw up, you let up, they'll boo. And they're right to do it. I think the people made me better than what I was. You understand what I'm saying? They were for me and they made me feel like a millionaire. There's no place like home. You know where my home is? Chicago.

Ralph Kiner

Ralph Kiner led the National League in home runs seven consecutive seasons before being dealt to the Cubs in 1953 to be teamed with another power-hitting outfielder, Hank Sauer. Center fielder Frankie Baumholtz had to cover a lot of territory between the two. Neither Kiner nor Sauer were known for their speed, and Kiner says he'd beat Sauer in a footrace any day. Funny, but Sauer says he could outrun Kiner. Anyway, Kiner loved Chicago but disputes a story that Baumholtz once caught a ball in foul territory. Kiner also challenges Phil Cavarretta's claim about who got the Cubs to eliminate seats in center field and install a dark hitter's background at Wrigley Field. Kiner joined the Mets as a broadcaster in 1962 and had a front row seat to the '69 pennant race.

If Frankie did that [caught a ball in foul territory], he didn't do it when I was there. He was a good center fielder. Sauer was the left fielder and when I came, they moved him to right. He resented the fact that he was demeaned about his defensive ability. I don't think neither one of us was as slow as everyone thought. When you hit home runs, you don't have to be fast.

I enjoyed playing for the Cubs. Of all the cities in the east, that's my favorite by far. And the fact that you could play all day games, which I loved. The only problem with that was that it was really a tough park to hit in because the fans were in center field and they were wearing white shirts and it was really difficult to find the ball.

In a game at Wrigley, you could have four at bats and you'd lose six or seven pitches that you'd never see. If they happened to be at your head, you didn't have time to get out of the way. All the players in the National League were complaining about the fact that it was tough to see the ball with all the white shirts out there.

I was the player rep for the National League. I went to Jim Gallagher, who was the general manager at the time, and I made a presentation that they make a change. His response was that it would cost the Cubs a lot of money because they'd lose the seats.

We weren't drawing a lot of people at that time. From a legal standpoint, I was the guy who got it done. Cavarretta had nothing to do with it.

You'll never believe this, but at one time, Ernie [Banks] never said one thing. When he joined the Cubs, he was really a quiet guy and obviously he had a lot of talent but was very raw. He gives me credit—although I don't think I had much to do with it—but he gives me credit for helping him learn about major league pitchers. He was a shortstop then. At that time, he was really a pretty raw player, but he, of course, developed into one of the great ones.

I remember in spring training we used to talk a lot about what the pitchers were trying to do, and trying to get him out, and the things he had to learn about the opposing pitchers, and what have you. It was something he didn't have any idea about. When you look at that ballclub, we had a lot of talent. We just didn't have enough pitching to carry us through.

I don't remember anybody getting on Ernie Banks at all. Let's put it this way—they didn't get on him any more than they did on any of the rest of us. Ernie was just a player coming in and the Cubs had Gene Baker at second base. It wasn't that big a deal. He did handle it well, whatever there was, but by '53 it was not unusual to have half black players on the field.

We had Sauer and Ransom Jackson, and Cavarretta was the manager. He was the first guy to ever get fired in spring training. He went in to see Wrigley and I guess they asked, "Where is this team going to finish?" and he said, "Last." And Wrigley didn't think that was too smart and that's the reason he got fired. He was a hard-nosed player and a great one. Then Stan Hack took over the job. He was a very easygoing guy and a good guy to have around. Phil hated to lose and he was very honest, and that was the reason he got fired.

One thing I remember about Hank—every time he did well they would shower him with tobacco in right field. Bags of tobacco. He chewed tobacco. When I hit a home run, they'd throw Wrigley spearmint gum to me. I tried tobacco once and got so sick, I never did it again.

Hank was the No. 1 favorite, there's no question about that. When I came, it was with mixed emotions, because in '52, Hank and I tied for the home run championship. When I got there in '53, maybe there was fan resentment against me that I was going to replace him.

We used to pal around together. We went to this place in Chicago, Eli's, and that's where all the players used to hang out. I still go there. It was a real political hangout. All the top politicians would hang out there.

It was common for all the guys to get together and pal around together. Now they don't do that. We did it because we traveled by train and the team was always together. You'd have your own private dining car, and talk baseball, and play cards, or whatever. It was like family talk.

Did anybody tell you about the psychologist? It was '53 or '54, and Wrigley called in a psychologist to talk to the players. We had to attend these lectures about the "will to win" and how you should think. I remember one player, who was not really a star but a player on the team, and as this psychologist was talking about how you're a pitcher on the mound, you've got to think about getting that batter out. We're sitting there listening and I'm thinking, this is junk. This one guy said, "What if you're pitching to Stan Musial and he thinks he can hit you?" That was the end of the meeting.

Sixty-nine was a unique year, in as much as the Cubs were dominating baseball and the Mets were coming from nowhere. One thing I remember was [Ron] Santo, and Dick Selma, and some of the other guys were really exuberant about anything they did to help the team against the Mets.

There's one game I remember extremely well. The Mets were close at that time, they were maybe in second place trying to pass the Cubs. They came to New York and Bill Hands was the pitcher for the Cubs. When Tommie Agee came to the plate, he was knocked down by Hands. It was serious. It was on purpose. [Leo] Durocher was the manager then and he was famous for that. Jerry Koosman was the pitcher for the Mets, and when Santo came up—I think it was the second inning and he was batting fourth and the first hitter up—Koosman threw a pitch and if Santo hadn't thrown his arm up, he would've been hit in the head. Beanball pitching was common in those days. The Mets were making a statement.

I'll never forget that. I was broadcasting the game. The animosity between the Mets and Cubs in '69 was very strong.

Cub fans now are really amazing. They're the greatest fans in the world. After all these years, they haven't won a World Series since, what, 1908? I love to go to games in Chicago, and I think one of the reasons it's so popular is that it's still a game in the daytime. All the ambience is there with the people in the stands and the fans outside. To me, it's what baseball is all about. It's fun to be at the ballpark.

I read a lot about the reason the Cubs have not been successful is that they play all day games. In my mind, it's a great asset. You have a wonderful routine of life. I didn't want to be traded away from Pittsburgh, but the chance to go to the Cubs was not bad. I really enjoyed playing in Chicago.

When I was there, Wrigley's philosophy was that you could come to the ballpark any day. There were no advance ticket sales. It was like going to a game in the playgrounds. You could come in, and watch the game, and have fun.

Eddie Miksis

Perhaps Eddie Miksis's greatest claim to Cubs fame is that he loaned Ernie Banks his glove for Banks's first game at shortstop. The utility infielder was acquired in a seven-player trade on June 15, 1951, between the Cubs and Brooklyn that cost Chicago popular center fielder Andy Pafko. The Dodgers got the better of the deal. Miksis stayed in Chicago from 1951 to 1956, starting at second base when he first arrived before being replaced by Gene Baker. The catcher whom Miksis can't remember is Rube Walker. Most Cub fans probably can't recall him, either, but maybe they can laugh as Miksis reminisces.

Let me tell you, I was traded from the Dodgers to the Cubs. The Dodgers were in Chicago for a weekend series and we just changed uniforms and clubhouses. Bruce Edwards, Joe Hatten, Gene Hermanski, and me they traded for Andy Pafko, [Johnny] Schmitz, Wayne Terwilliger, and a catcher. I can never remember his name. They called him "Popeye," I think.

They said, "We made a trade, you're a Chicago Cub." My roommate, Bruce Edwards, took it real hard. We were staying in a hotel in Chicago. He was just gazing out the window. He couldn't understand it. We had tremendous camaraderie on that Brooklyn Dodgers ballclub. When I was traded, we had a 14½-game lead in the National League. The deadline of the trade was June 15 or whatever. We had such camaraderie, we would've won that championship in the National League by at least 20, 25 games. They traded the camaraderie away for Andy Pafko and Johnny Schmitz, but guess what? That's the year Bobby Thomson hit the home run. You know, "The Giants win the pennant, the Giants win the pennant." That one. They hit it off one of my roommates, Ralph Branca. And I went from a first-place ballclub to a second-division ballclub.

I never felt the same camaraderie on the Cubs. I guess because the Dodgers were a winning ballclub and the Cubs were a totally different organization. The Dodgers treated you like kings, and I'll give you an example. We had just come from spring training in Mesa, Arizona, and we're coming into Chicago for a series with the White Sox prior to opening the season. All the bulletin boards say, "Be at Comiskey Park at 11:30," but no transportation. So, the players approached me and asked me if I would ask Phil Cavarretta if there was going to be any transportation. If not, we'll hire a bus. Nobody had cars. Is everybody going to take a cab to Comiskey? That'll cost a bundle. So I went into Phil's office and said, "Can I use your phone?"

He said, "What are you doing?"

I said, "I'm calling Greyhound bus lines. We're going to rent a bus to go to Comiskey Park. I'm just trying to save us some money." They hire limousines to take them today.

Phil took the phone and hung it up on me. He got hold of the traveling secretary. And I got the handle of being the clubhouse lawyer. It got back to certain writers like Jim Enright. It was a total disgrace. But we got the bus. And guess what? The Cubs didn't charge us. I was shocked at that. I thought they'd take it out of our meal money.

Every year since I've been out of baseball, I received a Christmas card. Guess from who? The Baltimore Orioles. And I only played 30 days with them. The Brooklyn Dodgers sent me cards the last five, six, seven years. The Chicago Cubs? Never.

Phil was a very no-nonsense guy. He was a hard-headed guy. Win under any costs. He was a good, hard-headed ballplayer. When I was with the Cubs, we had the best swearing ballclub in the National League. Profanity. I am not kidding you. We had Cavarretta, Don Hoak, and Dee Fondy. There was an old couple who had box seats right behind the dugout and they couldn't take it anymore. We ran them right out of the ballpark. Every other word. It was awful.

The first game Ernie Banks ever played in, he used my glove. It's in his book. He left his glove wherever he came from. Gene

Baker was there, too. It became the Banks and Baker combination. I played all positions, I played third, short, second, and one season out in center field. You know what I didn't like about playing center field? Running back and forth after every inning.

When I was with the Cubs, I had Dee Fondy at first base. You might as well have had a statue out there. He'd misplay a throw or something, and he'd say, "E-6" or "E-4." Not him, though. He was a butcher.

[Roy] Smalley was a mechanical shortstop. When he caught a ball, he had a 1-2-3 throw. He couldn't throw from the hole. Your second baseman almost got killed on the back of double plays. He had a tremendous arm, one of the best arms in baseball.

Chuck Connors was a hell of an athlete. A big-time basketball player in the NBA—New York Knicks I think he played for. He was in the Dodgers organization. He led that league with Montreal damn near every year in hitting, but when he came up to the major leagues, he couldn't buy a hit. They traded him to the Cubs and he must have broke a bat every time he went to bat. They jammed him on his fists. One day, during a game, I'm in the outfield and he's on his knees looking up at the sky. He says, "God, I gave you $5 in the collection. Please God, let me get a base hit."

He used to quote "Casey at the Bat" on the bus. Tucson to Mesa, Mesa to Tucson. It got to be where he should've been an actor before he was a ballplayer. We'd go into a restaurant, four of us together, and if there was an empty mike on the stage, he'd turn around and start quoting "Casey at the Bat." He was tremendous. He was a good actor. We'd go to the movies and he always had a water gun on him. When he was sitting up in the upper deck, he'd find some bald-headed guy.

Hank Sauer was a good, long ball hitter. Can you imagine this outfield? We had Frankie Baumholtz in center, and Ralph Kiner in left, and Sauer in right field. Ground balls that would go through the shortstop's legs were automatic doubles. Unbelievable. That's the truth.

I remember one thing about Randy Jackson. We had a 154-game schedule and after the first ballgame, he'd say, "One hundred fifty-three to go." He wasn't too enthusiastic.

[Sammy] Sosa's wearing my number now: 21. I'm surprised Yosh [Kawano] never retired my number. He gave it to a pretty good ballplayer.

Ernie Banks

In 1953, Gene Baker and Ernie Banks became the first two African American players on the Cubs. Banks, a slender shortstop who had played for the Kansas City Monarchs, made his major league debut on September 17 and stayed in the lineup for 424 games, a record start-up. In 1955, he was the first major league shortstop to hit 40 home runs, and in '58, Banks led the league in homers with 47. He won the Most Valuable Player Award that year—the first time it was presented to someone from a losing team—and repeated as Most Valuable Player in '59 with 45 homers and 143 runs batted in. Banks would hit the ball over the fences with relative ease, using his strong forearms and a relatively light, thin-handled, 31-ounce bat. Leo Durocher arrived in '66, and Banks's team-mates said the manager was jealous of the popular first baseman. But Banks compliments Durocher's style. In 1970, Banks hit his 500th home run, and he entered the Hall of Fame in 1977. He is Mr. Cub.

Gene and I didn't talk very much about things when we arrived here. We just introduced ourselves and then introduced ourselves to other players. We just came out on the field and went about our business and started taking ground balls. Talking was not a big part of our lives when I first came here. I got that from Jackie Robinson. First time I walked on the field, he came across over to third base, and he said, "I'm glad to see you here, and I know you can make it. You've got a lot of ability. Just listen." And that's what I did.

I was a listening person and that's all I knew when I first came here, just to listen to people and what they're talking about. Lot of interviews, you know—Milo Hamilton and Jack Brickhouse—and many pregame shows and postgame shows. I didn't know what to say. I always felt embarrassed about the questions. "How do you feel today?" "What did you hit yesterday?" "What do you think about this?" I didn't know how to deal with that. It was a learning process for me. Jackie prepared me for what it would be like. It's not that I was afraid of it. I just didn't understand the communication of the people who followed the game. I came from the Kansas City Monarchs, and all I knew was just to go play.

Gene was the same way. We came out of the same background, although he was a little bit older. We got on the field and we learned by just watching other people. Watching Monte Irvin, watching Willie Mays, watching some of your own players—Hank Sauer, Ralph Kiner. Just by watching. I didn't play in the minor leagues. If I had to sum it all up, it was just beautiful to learn as much as you could by listening and learn how to play the game.

I would see a few people in the stands at the time I started here. I had an interesting career because at the beginning of my career, very few people came. Toward the end of my career, more people came. Then we had several systems of managers here that didn't affect me at all because I was just listening to them talk about things and philosophies.

Phil Cavarretta was my first manager and he was a playing manager and he said very little. When I played my first game, he said, "You're playing shortstop today." We were standing around the batting cage, and I just shook my head and that was it.

Then we went to Stan Hack and we had Bob Scheffing, we had the rotating coaches system, we had Bob Kennedy, we had Lou Boudreau, Charlie Grimm. Then Leo came in 1966, so that's when the excitement and the energy began to develop. At that time I was 38, 39, and toward the end of my career, and it was really exciting to see more people in the stands, to see more energy, to see the media who had kind of backed away from the Cubs in the early days, how they got more involved to cover the Cubs and interview Leo. At that time, the manager was the key person and they interviewed the manager rather than the players.

My career here has been two sides. The two sides of playing before small crowds, playing in a park where Pat Peiper just said, "Play ball." There was no music. The national anthem only played on special days because Mr. Wrigley believed in that. [Then later in my career the Cubs introduced] music and singing the national anthem every day and Pat Peiper on the P.A. giving the announcements and the lineups. It was like going from the beginning of time to the modern times.

The modern times were when the lights came and a lot of other changes came in the promotional and marketing stuff. Mr. Wrigley didn't believe in a lot of the promotional days because he felt, in just listening to him, that you were creating situations where you were actually paying people to come to see you play. That's how he figured it.

It's been an education. I look at Wrigley Field as really a university for me, learning about different kinds of people, different cultures, different philosophies, and all of the above.

Now, getting back to Leo. He brought the energy to the organization in many ways, by excitement and creativity and fear. Most people kind of belabor the fact that he didn't like me or I didn't like him. It's a normal thing—I've learned this from my own family, and I come from a family of 12—it's a normal thing to kind of create discord between people. But I never allowed it because I learned many years ago that whoever was the boss is in charge, and I respected that. Most people thought Leo didn't like me and I didn't like him. I never met a person I disliked. That's my philosophy. The players didn't know it, some of the fans didn't know it, the media didn't know it. It didn't matter to me. He was the boss, he was the manager. That was his job. My message to players is whoever is in charge is the boss.

If I was on the bench, I'd always sit by him because I'd learn from him. When I was on the plane, I'd always sit by him. I'd always sit by him on the bus. To me, it was a learning experience just being around him. I went to his wedding, and it was just wonderful to see the joy in his life when he married Lynn Goldblatt.

I spent time with him in California, I was with him at times when he went to see the Dean Martin show and all that. My life, that most people didn't see on a day-to-day basis, was a learning experience with him. Then when he retired and I retired, Marvin Davis asked me to bring an All-Star team to Denver of the best players who'd played in the major leagues. I got all these players together—Willie Mays, Hank Aaron, Sandy Koufax, all of them—for an exhibition game in Denver. I wanted Leo and Gene Mauch to manage. I called Leo in Palm Springs, woke him up. He said, "What are you calling me for?"

I said, "Well, I need a favor, Leo. I've got this team together in Denver and I'd like for you to be the manager."

He said, "I don't want to come up there, Ernie. C'mon. The writers will be on me. I've had enough of that stuff."

I said, "Leo, it's going to be a nice thing, it's going to help to get baseball in Denver."

He said OK.

I said, "We'll make all the arrangements."

And he came. I got Gene Mauch, and they came and they had the greatest time of their lives. They had 50,000 people at the stadium. I still remember that. It was a real joy.

Many of the players didn't quite understand my own philosophy. I believe in forgive and forget, and keep your mouth shut and listen to whatever somebody is trying to tell you and you can learn something. I tell my children that. But it was just misinterpreted that Leo disliked me. He made my life better, he made me a better player.

I remember, in St. Louis, I hit two home runs and drove in seven runs one time against Steve Carlton. I mean, there's many things I was proud of. I was the oldest player on the team at 39 years old. Most people wouldn't even have been on the team at that time. But [Leo] inspired me to reach inside of myself and do more. And that's what I did. I had over 100 RBI and 20 and 30 home runs. Most people said, "Well, he has enough." It was just inspiration to let somebody know that somebody in your life—it could be a wife, it could be a manager, it could be a coach—could light your fire, that would stimulate your life and that's what happened to me when Leo came here from '66 to '72.

One of the more famous things—for the players, not me—was a fly ball hit up between first and second in St. Louis. The ball dropped and we lost the game, so Leo had a meeting afterward and I was the culprit of that whole thing. He kept us in the locker room about an hour or so, and he was just talking about the way I played and everything he said was right. He said, "You're a veteran player, you've got to go catch the ball. I mean, c'mon, my momma could've caught that ball" and, you know, different things. All the players were there listening. When we were released to go, many of the players were inspired in many ways. They said, "If he can get on Ernie Banks, who's a veteran player, he can get on anybody. Me, too." That was the purpose of it.

I just figured there are certain motivations that people have, especially if they're leaders, to get people to do more and Leo did that for me. I don't think anybody mentions this, but we had a Randy Hundley fantasy camp. I was there the first year and Leo came one year. And he said, "Ernie was a guy who really helped. I want to apologize for all the things maybe you guys have heard about." All of them were real shocked.

Sometimes people like to see others persecuted in some way. It's just human nature, you know. They like to see somebody get beat down by somebody else. I always felt in my life and my experiences with people that I got better just by listening and being around people like Buck O'Neil, and Satchel Paige, and Josh Gibson, and Gene Baker, and Monte Irvin, and Jackie Robinson—guys who were older than me—saying, "This is where you have to go. You have to listen and learn and go do your job. Just do your job. Not a whole lot of talking." That's what I've always believed in in my own life and my own career. Just do my job. That's all I thought of.

But Leo was surely a big influence toward the end of my career. I can think of so many incidents where he put life into it. We're playing in New York. John Bocabella was playing at first base—Leo had just made that announcement—and the first play of the game, John hurt his arm tagging a runner out. Everybody went out, and I just got up and started throwing. When Leo turned around to look, I was the only one there that he could see, so I went in the game and hit a home run.

Another time—one of the most touching things that ever happened to me—again in New York, we were losing the game and Leo sent up Jim Hickman to pinch-hit for me. As we were passing, Jim said, "Ernie, I'm sorry I'm doing this." He apologized for pinch-hitting for me. Leo didn't hear it, nobody else heard it. I didn't want to embarrass him. I just looked up and said, "You can do it." And I went on back to the dugout. It didn't bother me. What I'm saying is, embarrassment and unkind things that we all must learn from really can make us better—better people, better individuals.

Overall, my life here has been a learning process from the beginning to the day I retired when Whitey Lockman was the manager. It's just learning something every day from some young fan or some older fan. Everywhere I go, there's somebody that has touched my life and I have touched their lives. They were 10 years old sitting out there in those bleachers. Now they're in their 50s and they start talking to me about the experiences they had at Wrigley Field and the joy they had in watching me play. I don't remember all of it, but they do. It really is a good feeling to know that you touched people's lives that you don't even know you're touching and how important it is. Some of them are doctors, lawyers, CIA agents, FBI agents, some are presidents of companies.

What I always thought of when I walked out of this ballpark when I was playing was that one day I might have to ask this little boy or girl for a job. I always thought of that. I don't know why. My children would say, "Dad, we got to go." And I'd be signing autographs, looking at faces. I thought, gosh, I might ask you for a job someday or you might have to save my life. I always thought of that. I can't explain it. I always had empathy for people who came to Wrigley Field.

My whole experience here was based on empathy. I always felt what other people felt. Same way with the players I played with. We had many different kinds of players, many different kinds of managers, from every kind of culture around, and you have to understand that and mix in and just listen to them. Even how they felt in certain situations when they first came up.

Billy Williams, when he first came up, he really wanted to quit. He got disillusioned, and Buck O'Neil and I went to see him at Northwestern Hospital. Buck was doing most of the talking. He said, "Hey, Billy, you missed a great game today," and Billy came back and got inspired and went out and won Rookie of the Year that year. It's all about that. About having someone to light your fire, to get you moving, to let you know you have a lot more to give, a lot more to do. It's tied into hard work, it's tied into discipline, it's tied into attitude.

All the players I played with, I loved those guys like brothers. I stay in touch with them. That's my thing now, staying in touch with the people I spent time with here at Wrigley Field. They're like an extended family. I'm really concerned about their children. My children grew up with them, Billy's children, Santo's children, Hundley's children. It's just a wonderful environment. I wish everybody could experience the kind of things I experienced in my life and am still experiencing.

"Let's Play Two." That started in '69. Like most things, it just kind of come out. It was July and over 100 degrees, and everybody was kind of down a little bit. I came in the locker room and Jimmy Enright was there and a lot of writers were around, and I said, "Boy, this is a great day. Let's play two."

They all woke up and looked around, and it stayed with me for a long while. Then we played a doubleheader in Houston, and me and Lou Brock fell out in the first game of the doubleheader. It was about 120 degrees in Houston. I hit a double and fainted, and Lou Brock hit a triple and fainted. They took us out and ever since then, most of my friends around the league always remember that. "You always want to play two, but what happened that day in Houston?"

The great joy in my life is to come out to Wrigley Field now. Coming out here is better than going to a psychiatrist. It's real therapy for me. The other parks are OK, but it's special coming here. The people are enthusiastic. They really love this park, and they love the players, and they love everything about it. It's the epicenter of all our lives, and that's why I enjoy coming here so much.

I hope they don't change it. I'm sure there will come a time when there will be some changes. The lights are up. They'll probably have advertising, they'll probably have a bigger ballpark to get more people. To me, it's just a wonderful place to be and I really love it.

Wrigley Field is such an important part of people's lives. It really is, worldwide. I was walking down the street in Hong Kong and met people [who asked about it]. Went to the Vatican and had an audience with the pope in '69, and he's talking about Wrigley Field.

Most people I've been around in my life, now naturally in their 50s or 60s, their lives have been touched by Wrigley Field. Their memories are long-lasting and have no age. They can remember the first time coming here, and what happened, and who was playing, and whether it was a cold day or whether it was a cloudy day.

Cub fans are highly intelligent people who really think [about the game]. They used to keep score here. When I first came, every fan—there weren't that many—they used to keep score. It's a thinking audience that understands and deals with logic and not make-believe stuff. It's dealing with what's happening now.

Don't criticize management. I learned from Mr. Wrigley that he didn't have season tickets when I first came here because he felt season ticket holders would be telling him how to run the team. He'd have 22,000 tickets that would go on sale the day of the game, so if people decided to come, they could just come to Wrigley Field. He established that a long time ago. He had Ladies Days and Senior Citizens Day and different days to encourage people to be a part of it. It kind of built up to where we are now, the generations have all been a big part of this wonderful team, this wonderful organization.

I liked what [Don] Baylor said when he came as manager. He said, "I'm happy to be managing for an organization that has been around for 100 years." Normally, people don't laugh at the Cubs because we haven't won since 1945. The Mets, they laugh at and they laugh at some of the other teams about how unsuccessful they are, but it's not funny to Cub fans. Cub fans don't get riled up. We just understand that they all are champions. A champion is the last one standing. All the people then and now, they're really champions. I think more teams should emulate and build toward the kind of fans who come here. They last a long time.

My contract was all private stuff. John Holland and Wid Matthews, they'd say we weren't drawing very much and I got criticized a lot for that from my own family and friends. They said, "You should be making more money." I didn't say anything. I just listened. They said it, but I didn't listen to them because playing here—if you can get the feeling in your own heart of playing for the love of it—then your life is better. That's the way it is here. Playing for the love of it, then your life will be better and your career will be better.

I know everybody else talks about all these other things. I wasn't around when they talked about the money part of the game. You approach playing at Wrigley Field for the love of it, and the other part is the friendship that you build when you're here. The friendships you make while you're here are much greater than all the money you will make in your life.

Speaking of the love of Wrigley Field, I was checking into Canyon Ranch, a famous health spa in Tucson, Arizona, and a nurse walked up to me. "Could you do me a favor? My grandfather was a longtime Cub fan and before he died, he wanted his ashes spread at Wrigley Field. Do they do that there?"

And I said, "I don't know, but I'll let you know before I leave."

So, I called, and they said, "Well, Ernie, we get a lot of requests from people who want to do that. We don't publicize it because we don't want to make it sound like a cemetery."

I know we haven't played well, but it's not a cemetery, so I told [the nurse] that. She said, OK, but I really wanted it to happen.

So now, I want it to happen for me. I want my ashes to be spread over Wrigley Field with the wind blowing out.

Moe Drabowsky

Moe Drabowsky and Dick Drott were 21 and 22 years old, respectively, in 1957. The right-handed rookies, a.k.a. the Gold Dust Twins or the Dandy Ds, worked together to win 28 games that season for the Cubs. Each struck out 170 batters. They were two of the few bright spots for the Cubs at that time. Unfortunately for Drott, he hurt his arm in '58 and was never the same. Drabowsky left the Cubs after the 1960 season, gratefully missing the college of coaches experience, and went on to total 54 saves for five different teams. But Drabowsky was more than a pitcher. He was a prankster.

I came up at the tail end of '56, right out of college, and back then you couldn't sign until your class graduated from college or you became 21 years old. So, at 21, I was a junior in college and then I signed with the Cubs at the end of July. I came to the big leagues and I spent six weeks here, then I told them I wanted to go back to college and complete my senior year. I didn't want to lose any college time. I left the ballclub early to go back to school. They said that was fine. Nowadays, guys get pampered with clubhouse suites.

After going to classes a couple weeks, the Cubs were coming into New York to play the Giants in the Polo Grounds, and I told my buddies I was pitching Tuesday. In the third inning, I was gone. The guys hadn't arrived at the ballpark yet and I was gone.

Dick Drott came up the next year. We were the "Dandy Ds." We both threw effectively. I won 13 for a last-place club. We got a lot of notoriety. We both tied for second place in strikeouts in the National League.

We used to have our traveling secretary up in the scoreboard stealing signs. Don Biebel was his name. You've got all the little squares in the scoreboard and he'd be sitting way back in the squares. If he put his foot in the right-hand corner, that meant fastball. The hitter would just look up toward the pitcher and look past him at the scoreboard and see the squares, and if he sees a foot, he's ready to jump on a fastball. We might score nine runs or so and then lose 12–9, 13–10.

We didn't know we weren't a good team because we had Ernie Banks on the team. He was the supreme optimist. Let's play two, let's play two. Then we'd lose 8–2, then the next day, "Good day for baseball. Let's play two." We thought, what's wrong with this nut? Let's see, Ernie Banks might have been making $80,000 a year. I was making $6,000 a year, so if the situation were reversed, I might think the same.

When you're young and innocent—innocent from a baseball standpoint—you don't realize what it means to pitch at Wrigley Field with the wind blowing out. You come to the ballpark and check the flags—that's the first thing you do. When you're young, you want to be a starter. You don't like life in the bullpen. We thought bullpenners were second-rate citizens.

I always had a penchant for getting on the phone. In Milwaukee County Stadium, you can get an outside line in the bullpen. I was a stockbroker in the off-season, and I'd get an outside line and talk to some broker friends of mine. I was getting stock quotes one day. Poor Glen Hobbie. Here come Eddie Matthews, Hank Aaron, Frank Thomas. They're trying to get somebody to warm up in the bullpen. I'm sure the manager figured he must have gotten the wrong number. He kept getting "beep, beep, beep" on the phone. Then a couple guys get up in front of the dugout steps waving towels like semaphore signals. I was probably responsible for Hobbie's earned run average being higher than it should have been.

In Wrigley, if you hit a ground ball past third base fair, then it sometimes rolled to the gutter along the brick wall. One of the interesting things we did was right at the bullpen bench. We'd always drop our gloves in that gutter [when the opposition was at bat] so if a ball came in there, the ball would stop right where the gloves are so the outfielder could retrieve the ball. So, when we're hitting, we take the gloves out. One day, Tony Taylor hits a ball past third and the ball goes into the gutter and it scoots down there and goes all the way down the left field line. We're showing Orlando Cepeda where the ball is and we're watching Tony Taylor round the bases. Tony got an inside-the-park ground ball home run.

In San Francisco, when I was with the Cubs, Charlie Grimm was the manager and we had a 5–2 lead in the eighth. Seth Morehead was pitching against the Giants. Top of the eighth and we're hitting, and I'm kind of in the manager's doghouse—I'm not pitching too well. I go down to the left field bullpen to keep loose and stay in shape. In the bullpen, you throw toward the home plate area, just like at Wrigley Field. I had just released a pitch and I see this ball coming toward me, so I backhand this ball. I'd just let a pitch go and I fielded it. Well, it was a ball hit past third base and it had gone into foul territory. Frank Thomas hit it, it's a sure double, maybe a triple, but because I fielded the ball the umpires have a big conference and they don't know what to do. They decide to rule it a single. Don Zimmer comes up and gets a base hit. It would've scored Frank Thomas from second. We don't score a run. We have a 5–2 lead, and the Giants come up and two guys get on, and Willie McCovey comes up and he hits one nine miles; it's a three-run homer and now it's 5–5. Fortunately, we won the game in 10 innings, 6–5. If we'd lost that game I'd have felt badly enough. Charlie Grimm said if we had lost that game, my bags would've been packed that night.

One other play comes to mind. Stan Musial was the hitter. This was the most unusual play I've seen in major league baseball. The count goes to three balls, two strikes. Bob Anderson is the pitcher. There's a fastball in on the hands. Musial doesn't swing, but I hear a sound, like a tick. There's a sound and the ball goes back to the screen. So Musial takes off for first base. Sammy Taylor is the catcher and he thinks it's a foul ball, so he puts his hand back behind his shoulder and the umpire sees that and pops him another ball. Musial sees the ball back near the screen and he takes off for second. Nobody's covering at second and Taylor sees Musial running, so he throws the ball he got from the umpire and the ball goes out into center field. Musial goes on to third. Alvin Dark comes in from third and he goes back to the screen to retrieve the ball. Well, Pat Peiper, the public address announcer, had gone over to pick up the ball and put it in the ball bag. So, Dark goes to the ball bag and pulls out a ball and throws it to Banks who's covering at third. And all of a sudden—boom—Banks tags Musial at third. Well, the umpires had a long conference with that one, 10 or 15 minutes. Finally, they called Musial out because that ball that was in center field was the ball that was in play.

We had no clue. I'm not sure if the ball was put in the ball bag. Somebody said they saw Pat Peiper do that. The umpires were looking at the play out in fair territory. It was a crazy, crazy play.

I played in the major leagues for 17 years. That's probably the biggest prank I've pulled, surviving that long. You come up as a starting pitcher, you like that. Then you hurt your arm and the ball doesn't move as much, and the velocity's not as good, and then you've got to survive. You really don't learn a heck of a lot about pitching until you hurt your arm. A lot of guys think it's a piece of cake. You talk to Cal Ripken, Wade Boggs. I don't think any of those guys think it's a piece of cake.

Glen Hobbie

After he pitched a game for the Cubs, Glen Hobbie would take a shower and go home. No ice packs, no rubdowns, no special treatment. "The only guy I know who used ice at that time was Sandy Koufax," said Hobbie, who pitched for the Cubs from 1957 to 1964. The big right-hander shut out Cincinnati in his first major league start May 6, 1958, and he won 16 games in back-to-back seasons in 1959 and 1960. But Hobbie also lost 20 games in 1960. He held St. Louis to one hit on April 21, 1959, retiring the first 20 batters he faced. The Cardinals' Stan Musial got the only hit, but Hobbie got revenge later in the game and, more important, the win.

I have one flashback to that game, the one-hitter. Sammy Taylor called for a fastball to Musial, and I shook him off and threw a curve, and Musial got a hit. But you know Musial getting that one hit didn't affect my life. I can remember exactly where the pitch was. It was higher than I wanted. I wanted it down below the knees and I got it waist high. It barely cleared the left field chalk line about three inches. What no one remembers is in that same game in the ninth inning with two outs, I walked somebody, the score was still 1–0. Somehow, the runner ended up on second base and Musial came up again. He's at the plate again and he hits a ground ball back to me, and I throw him out, so I got him out when I had to.

Look at the complete games I had in 1960. How many times do you do that? Sixteen games. Usually you don't have that many for a whole team. I pitched an awful lot. I had guys on other ballclubs say, "Hobbie, they're going to ruin you." I don't think that was it. I just burned out at the end of the year. I lost 20 because I was in the game long enough to get a decision.

There was a Friday when I pitched eight innings against St. Louis and got beat, and came back to the ballpark Sunday morn-

ing and they said, "You're pitching on one day's rest," and won
1–0. You did a lot of pitching back then. You did what you were
told to do.

We weren't worth three, four, five million dollars like they are
today. I'm not sorry. We made decent money back then. We didn't
make an overabundance of money. That game I pitched against St.
Louis when Musial got the one hit, I don't think there were 1,000
people in the stands. Baseball was just growing at that time. The
only time you really had super crowds was when you played St.
Louis in a weekend series or Milwaukee in a weekend series, and
that time you'd have 30,000, 34,000. We had some great ballplayers, too. One year we had five guys who hit 20 or more home
runs and Banks hit 44. We had exciting players to watch.

I watched Ernie and wondered how he could do it because he
did it so easy. He did it so effortlessly. It seemed like it was no
effort at all. When he hit a home run, it was just like he got a base
hit. He was super to watch.

Musial gave me trouble. I didn't have a whole lot of trouble
against Hank Aaron. The guys I had trouble with were usually the
contact hitters. The free swingers, I got out, the home run hitters. Probably the toughest guy I ever had to face was Frank
Robinson. He stood right on the plate. You couldn't get him out
inside or get him out outside. When I got him out, he nearly
killed an infielder.

Lou Boudreau

*When the Cubs began the 1960 season, Charlie Grimm was the man-
ager and Lou Boudreau was in the broadcast booth. The Cubs started
6–11 and were in last place when owner P. K. Wrigley traded Grimm
for Boudreau, moving the former star shortstop and Cleveland manager
from the booth to the dugout. But Boudreau couldn't work miracles, and
the Cubs went 54–83 to finish seventh. He then asked Wrigley for a
two-year contract, but the owner decided instead to experiment with the
college of coaches. Boudreau returned to the microphone in 1961, where
he stayed until 1989. He was elected into the Hall of Fame in 1970. He
died in August 2000 at the age of 84.*

I had inquired about being the manager of the Cubs. I put my
name up for being manager. I was fortunate enough to be named
manager, but then Col. Bob Whitlow suggested to Mr. Wrigley
to do what colleges do—hiring not one coach but several special
coaches. I did not agree and would not agree to a system of one
manager every two weeks. It would be different attitudes and
different styles. I was very fortunate that Mr. Ward Quaal, who
was president of WGN, asked me to come back and continue
broadcasting.

Charlie Grimm was great. He was great for the ballplayers, and
great for the fans, and great for the Cubs. He could play first base
and hit, of course. He was at a position where the Cubs were
lacking a good player until he came along. As a manager? Each
man has his own way of managing and his own thoughts about

managing, and that's why you could put three or four men together and their thoughts would be different. I think he was a good manager. He knew what he was doing. He was ahead of the play all the time. Even though when you say Charlie Grimm you think of a comedian and you think of someone who was perhaps lacking the ability to bear down or be tough on the ballplayers, but Charlie could. He loved to win. That's all you have to do.

I had to be careful criticizing from the radio booth. But I could criticize because of my experience on the field. I had the advantage. I figured out how to go about it. At times, you have to hold back and ease it in.

Things have changed not only on the ballfield, but in the radio booth. Broadcasters have to think about what they're saying and not say a lot to criticize. And now, they can see it on television. Years ago, you had radio and that was all.

You kept hoping that the Cubs would come through and have a winning streak, and get together and have a good season. It only takes two or three ballplayers to work together to make that happen. You live with it because you're with that team all the way.

I think the ballpark is very important to the Cubs. If they could get four or five individuals who were long fly ball hitters, they'd hit home runs. The Cubs do not hit and run and do not steal enough bases because they lack speed and they lack that type of hitter. Once you get those kind of hitters, you'll have a championship team.

Vince Lloyd

For 37 years, Vince Lloyd's voice was synonymous with the Cubs. He handled both radio and television broadcasts for WGN. Lloyd didn't have many opportunities to gush over the Cubs, but he relished his 18 seasons in the broadcast booth with Lou Boudreau. Lloyd got his break in a tragic way. Friend and broadcaster Jack Quinlan was killed in a car accident during 1965 spring training. Boudreau had to talk Lloyd into taking the job. Imagine Lloyd's baritone voice as he tells his story.

There were times when we'd leave spring training and we knew it was going to be a lousy ballclub. But we'd made up our minds that our job was to entertain, hopefully with a winning team. If they didn't win—and there were a lot of ballclubs that didn't—you still had to entertain the people. One of the best ways to do that was to keep them informed of what the game was all about and for that I relied on Lou a lot. We would sit up nights in spring training or on the road after a game just talking baseball and it led to a program, *Talk Baseball*, which I think is still on the air.

We'd go back to the hotel after a ballgame and a lot of times we'd share a suite. And we might sit up until 3:30, 4:00 in the morning, discussing different things that had happened, why they happened, why they didn't happen, just having fun talking about the game—not just about the game we'd seen, but the game of baseball in general. It led to some interesting discussions. It gave me a lot of knowledge that I didn't have prior to working with Lou.

He knew the game as a player, as a manager, and as a fan. I've been convinced from year to year that nobody—*nobody*—on the air ever had the knowledge that Lou had. He may not have always expressed it the best. Early on, when we worked together, I said, "Don't worry about your grammar or how you say something." He was a clean talker. I said, "You just say what's on your mind and I guarantee you any fan will know what you want to say."

And I think he did that superbly for the 18, 19 years that we worked together.

We used to work out together when nobody ever talked about working out together. We might play basketball or any other game one-on-one. Our studio was right across from the Wrigley Building and at the hotel next door, the Sheraton, they had a wonderful gym. We'd go over there at lunch hour and go after each other pretty good, and that was before we started working together.

I'd always admired him as a player and as a manager. I remember Bill Veeck telling me one time, I'd asked him about Lou as a manager. He tried to fire him one year and was smart enough to take a pass and Lou stayed. Veeck said, "He may not have been the greatest manager for strategy that I ever knew, but he was the greatest hunch player I've ever known in my life." He does that with the horses, too. And he's not broke yet.

I'd moved from television and working with Jack Brickhouse on both the White Sox and the Cubs, and they talked me into coming over to do the radio as Lou's partner. As a matter of fact, one of the things that persuaded me to move over was a call from Lou, and he said, "If you don't do the Cubs, I'll quit." I couldn't let that happen. We needed him.

I used to stop in their booth before a game to shoot the bull with him and Jack. We had good times together. I looked forward to working with him and we probably had as good a relationship as I could ever hope to have with anybody. He taught me a lot about the game. We thoroughly enjoyed it. We were lucky. We had some bad teams, but we had a lot of good ones, too. And we had outstanding players. I don't remember a single year that I covered the Cubs, going back into the early '50s, when there wasn't at least one outstanding player on that ballclub. That goes back to the days of Hank Sauer, Andy Pafko—there was just one after another. Of course, when Ernie came along, and Billy and Santo and that whole bunch, that was still my favorite ballclub—the

1969 Cubs team—even though they didn't win anything. If they had had a center fielder and one more relief pitcher, they'd have won it. No question about it. No team ever put out more than that '69 Cub team.

Jack Quinlan was a very dear friend of mine. He'd taken my place in Peoria when I left there to come to WGN. I introduced him to the gal who later became his wife. When he was killed in a car accident in spring training in Arizona, I was covering the state high school basketball tournament in Champaign. I remember going up to my room Friday night and calling home. I had started out of the room to meet a couple guys downstairs to have a beer, but I went back in to call the station. I don't know why, just to see if everything was all right. Before I hung up, the guy said, "Vince, you're going to get some bad news. You've lost a dear friend."

I said, "What happened? What are you talking about?"

He said, "Jack Quinlan was killed today in Arizona."

I couldn't believe it. He was coming back from a golf game with some mutual friends, and he missed the turnoff. At that time, the road split and went this way and that way. He started to go to the right and that was wrong, and he was going to cut across an intersection. There was a big semitrailer truck parked there, and he hit under that thing and was killed immediately.

He was probably the best baseball broadcasting talent I have ever heard to this day and a super, super guy. We had a lot of fun together on the golf course and at dinner at one another's homes. That was the big reason I did not want to take his job. I did not want to walk into that booth of his. Lou's remark to me on the telephone persuaded me that I'd better do it. It led to 19 or 20 wonderful years with him.

61

Don Zimmer

His cherubic face changes expression with every pitch. No one else can tell a story like Don Zimmer does, and he has many. He managed in San Diego, Boston, and Texas, but it wasn't until he arrived in Chicago to skipper the Cubs that he would finally win and with an unlikely bunch. They were the Boys of Zimmer. He also played for the Cubs in 1960–1961 when team owner Phil Wrigley decided to eliminate the manager's title and instead impose a rotating college of coaches. Zimmer will tell you how they did.

I went to the Cubs in '60 and '61. In '59, we won the World Series in L.A. Beat the White Sox. In '60, I got traded to the Cubs the last few days of spring training in Arizona. Charlie Grimm was the manager. We only had two days to play before we opened up in L.A., where I just got traded from. So, we got off to a bad start and I think they took Charlie Grimm and put him upstairs and brought down Lou Boudreau. We finished that year and the next year, and then they said, "We're not going to have a manager." It was like headlines in the Chicago papers. "We're going to have revolving coaches." The first thing I said was, "How the heck is that going to work?"

So, we go to spring training, and the way we were told it was probably going to work is that John Holland or Mr. Wrigley or whoever it might be, would tell the first guy, "You're the head coach, not manager. You're the head coach for 10 days or maybe two weeks." By rights, when his time was up, he was the revolv-

63

ing guy and would go down to Houston, which was our Triple-A club, and they'd bring somebody up. Then somebody else becomes the head coach for 10 days, two weeks.

The more I watched this, I said, "Boy, oh boy, how's this ever going to work?" First of all, when it's your time to manage for 10 days, what happens if you win 10 in a row? You'd stay, wouldn't you? They'd keep you. Well, how about the other guys? You think they're pulling for you? They're pulling against you, so they get a chance. There ain't no way everybody could be on the same page.

I can remember as this started, Santo was a young third baseman, a kid. One head coach, "Move back a little bit." Another one, "You got to move over a little bit." Another guy is telling him to come in. Finally, he said, "Let me play ball." He's got five guys telling him five different things. It was comical.

We opened up the season in Cincinnati, and they named Vedie Himsl as the head coach. Vedie Himsl has a meeting, and he says, "I talked to Mr. Wrigley and John Holland. Because we're going to have revolving coaches, we thought it would be a good idea to name a captain, and the captain will be Zimmer." Well, I was dumbfounded. What the hell is all this about? Vedie managed 10 days, two weeks, and I played every day, every inning. Then I think Harry Craft took over for 10 days and I played every day. Then I think Tappe took over and I played every day, this and that. Now the fourth guy—I may be off a time or two—but the fourth guy happened to be Lou Klein. We're leaving down in the corner of the clubhouse, and as we're walking out Lou Klein puts his arm around me and says, "I want you to be the pepper guy now in the infield and take charge," and this and that. I know I'm playing, for him to tell me that. I come up to see where I'm hitting and I ain't in the lineup. What's all the bullcrap you laid on me about being the holler guy? I never played in his eight or nine days, and I'm the captain.

Actually, the way it went, I think we lost 100 games or close to it. There were headlines in the paper, "Cubs Thought Revolving Coaches Worked. We'll Do It Again Next Year." Now this is the time at the end of the year where every club had to put seven guys on that expansion list for the New York Mets and somebody else. You had to put on two bonus choices, but you didn't have to put them on until after the World Series. I went to Elvin Tappe, who was a pretty good friend of mine, and I said, "Am I on that $75,000 expansion list?"

He said, "No, you're not on that."

I said, "Am I on the bonus choice?" You had to put two guys on, but you could only lose one of 'em for $125,000. "Am I on that?"

"No, you're not on that."

Now, Boudreau is the announcer. I'll never forget it. It was a Sunday morning, the last day of the season. Boudreau says to me, "I'd like to have you on the pregame show." I told Boudreau on the show, I said it was a popularity contest. "Three guys take over the job, I play every day, and Lou Klein comes in and I don't play an inning. If that's not a popularity contest, what is it?"

You got to remember that up in the clubhouse, the revolving coaches all listen to Boudreau's show every day. I'm already out on the field. So, I'll never forget Rip Collins came out to put his arm around me. He said, "I admire you. You never involved anybody else but yourself. I admire you for that."

Now, as I'm drifting up toward the dugout, Charlie Grimm is sitting up in the box seats. He's vice president. I always liked Charlie. He calls me over and I guess he heard the thing. He told me the same thing Rip Collins did. "I respect you, and I respect the way you feel. You probably will be elsewhere."

And I understood that. Well, what they did, they had two guys already on—I think they had Don Elston and Barney Schultz on the $125,000 list. They had them on early. Somebody told me that they took Elston off and put me on, and that's how I wound up with the Mets.

Did [revolving coaches] work? No, chrissakes. It was crazy. How could anything like that work? Jesus Christ. Give a guy a break. You lose 100 games and they say it worked. The whole thing didn't make sense. If anybody told you any different, some of them would have to be lying, I think.

I managed Boston, we had some great teams. Win 90 games, 91, 97, 99 games. We were in the pennant race every year, right down to the last week of the season, which is the thrilling part of baseball. I've been on some [teams] where you're done in July already, and that's not too much fun. We [the Cubs] went to spring training in '89. We can't win a game. I'll never forget, I went to the ballpark early one morning, like every morning, 7:30, and Jim Frey is right opposite the door there in that trailer. [Cubs president Don] Grenesko usually would come to the park at 12 noon. Well, at noon, half the day's work is already over, especially early in the spring. I said, "Well, I'll stop in and say hello to Jimmy this morning." It was 7:30, quarter to eight, and Grenesko was in there which was very unusual. We're playing terrible. He says, "Do we ever do any fundamentals? It don't look like they're trying." He's the president. What I wanted to say was, "If you'd get your ass out of bed, you could be watching fundamentals at 10:00." But I didn't want to do that because I respect him as the president.

We keep losing in spring training and so forth and so on. We're going to leave Arizona and go to Minnesota to play two exhibition games, then come to Chicago. Saturday afternoon, we play. Saturday night, Jimmy and I went out to dinner. Jimmy had a couple martinis and he says to me, dead serious, "You think there's any chance at all that this club could win 81 games and be .500?"

I think we'd wound up 7–22 in spring training or something ridiculous like that. I said, "Jimmy, if we play .500 this year, you and I will dance down Michigan Avenue together."

If we'd won in Boston—we were picked to win in Boston, either first or second—it would've been a big thing for me. But everybody picked the Cubs last. Everybody. And I think that's what made it more important and a bigger thrill for me, because nobody picked us and our guys played so good. Little things, they did every little thing. Even managing today, if I went to manage today, sometimes you get in a streak for 10 days and everything you do is right. All of a sudden, it flops. Then you back off because everything went haywire. Well, we had a season that everything went right. It was just absolutely amazing.

I've had a lot of thrills in the game, but winning the division in 1989, clinching it in Montreal, was the biggest thrill I've had in the game. And that includes winning World Series and hitting grand-slam home runs. That was my biggest thrill.

Buck O'Neil

In 1953, the Cubs hired Buck O'Neil as a scout, and his first assignment was to sign a young shortstop named Ernie Banks. In '62, O'Neil became the first African American coach in the major leagues, joining the Cubs' college of coaches. However, he never got a turn to manage or even go on the field for a game. In a Cubs–Houston game in '62, Charlie Metro, the manager of the moment, was ejected. Then, third base coach Elvin Tappe was tossed. That left Lou Klein to manage and no one to handle third base duties. O'Neil was on the bench—and stayed there. O'Neil calls it one of his greatest disappointments in baseball.

Charlie Metro later told me that Charlie Grimm had told them not to ever let me coach at third base. If I did, somebody was going to lose their job coaching at third base. Grimm had seen me work in spring training. He said he didn't want me coaching on the line.

That was a disappointment. All of the guys, they thought, "Buck's going to coach at third base now." But I was there on the bench. They got Fred Martin, who was the pitching coach, and brought him from the bullpen to coach, which left nobody down in the bullpen. All that just to keep me from coaching at third base, which was stupid.

The players were watching and they just shook their heads. They were very disappointed that it happened that way. Charlie Grimm was supposed to be my friend. It was sad.

I knew the Cubs were going to hire me. I'd signed Ernie Banks to the Monarchs. We played our East-West All-Star Game at Comiskey Park [in 1953], which we did every year. After the game, Tom Baird, who was the owner of the team, he called and said, "In the morning, I want you to bring Ernie out to the ballpark. The Cubs want to sign him." Wendell Smith, the writer, picked us up at the hotel and took us out to Wrigley Field.

Wid Matthews said, "Baseball is just about over in the Negro Leagues. When Tom sells this team, we'd like you to come work for the Cubs and scout for the Cubs."

I said, "Thank you very much."

And Wid Matthews said, "Since you signed Ernie to a Monarchs contract, you can sign Ernie to a Cubs contract."

Ernie was just a kid. He didn't say much. Not anymore. I think he got a lot of that from me. I spent a lot of time with him when he was with the Cubs.

Gene [Baker] was a pro. He had played for me before Ernie and before the Cubs signed him. He played in the Pacific Coast League for a few years. Gene was a shortstop and Ernie was a shortstop. So they thought the right thing to do was move the veteran ballplayer to second base and put Ernie at shortstop. The first time Gene played second base was in the major leagues.

I told them, just be a ballplayer, just like anybody else. As much as Ernie talks now, Ernie's shy. He is really shy. I think that's one of the reasons he talks quite a bit now.

When Lou Brock came up with the Cubs, that was the year I was a coach. We roomed together. I enjoyed living with Lou. But at the same time, Lou had a lot of friends out of Louisiana. He had gone to Southern University and a lot of those friends were in Chicago. They were so thrilled to be with Lou, and they'd be keeping Lou out late at night. I'd say, "C'mon, Lou, you got to come in earlier than that."

He'd say, "Why do I have an old man rooming with me?"

Billy Williams left the ballclub. That was in the minor leagues. He was in Texas and he went home. You know, this happens to kids, but usually when kids are having a hard time. He was leading the league when he left. They called me and said, "Billy's gone home. Go see what's wrong with him." I went over to visit with him, took him to dinner, said nothing about going back. They played a lot of baseball, semipro baseball around Mobile. I took him to a game and when we got to the field, they were so glad to see Billy. "Oh, Billy, we're so glad to see you. Man, I want to get to organized baseball so bad I can taste it."

I think he was a little homesick. He was in love, too, with his sweetheart. He had a little puppy love. The next day, he told me, "I'm ready to go back."

George Altman

George Altman is one of the most worldly Cubs. The big, powerful out-fielder played in Chicago for two stints, 1959–1962 and 1965–1967. He was an All-Star in 1961 and 1962 when he batted .303 and .318, respectively. Altman also spent a winter playing in Cuba and eight years in Japan. He was diagnosed with colon cancer in 1974 and played one more season in Japan before he eventually retired to become a stockbroker. He has since turned off his trading computer and now coaches baseball and offers legal advice. Altman had to endure the college of coaches experiment, but he also witnessed racial prejudice by Cubs management.

We probably didn't have a couple of the needed ingredients at the time, which was pitching and defense up the middle and also leadership. That was the time of the college of coaches, so it's leadership from the managerial point of view and also from the players' point of view. We didn't have a unified ballclub. There were cliques here and cliques there.

We scored runs, there's no doubt about that. But so did other teams. We didn't have good, consistent starting pitching and relief.

The college of coaches didn't bother me that much because I was playing every day in the lineup. It wouldn't affect everyday players that much. But the bench or the fringe players, one manager would evaluate a player differently than another manager.

I think another demoralizing thing was that Buck O'Neil was part of that and he was a great manager in the Negro Leagues and a very inspirational guy. He was waiting for his chance, which he never got. And that didn't sit well with the players either. He was a tremendous manager and motivator. He was known to get the most out of the players. He was the manager, like the old cliche goes, that players would run through a brick wall for. Vedie Himsl and Elvin Tappe—they didn't have any experience. Buck had a world of experience and the others didn't have any.

They put him on the bottom of the rotation and when it came up to his turn, they scrapped the whole deal. We talked about how he was going to get his turn. Charlie Metro was in charge and Buck kind of questioned his strategy. One time, Bobby Wine was at bat and Charlie decided to walk Bobby Wine or something like that and Buck said out loud, "The one you're pitching to is better than the one you walked."

Charlie said, "Never mind Buck, you'll get your turn later."

Buck was in line, but he just never got the opportunity. He had a big booming voice and when he told you to do something, you did it.

At that time, there's no doubt about it that there were limits as far as where the Cubs were going to go in terms of possibly players and as far as the management. I know one time we had a vote for the player representative and I was up for the vote against Bob Will. Tappe came in and said, "Mr. Wrigley wants Bob Will," and that was the end of it.

The white players had their own group and we had our own group, and there was no socializing after the game. We weren't able to stay in the same hotel as the white players initially in St. Louis, but within one year that was cleared up. Even though we were in the same motel, that was all. There was no lunch or dinner together. You go your way, I'll go mine.

Lou Brock was a raw talent that everybody knew was going to be a success. Anybody who had any experience in baseball knew it. All you had to do was look at the guy. He had blinding speed. He had hit .340 in the minor leagues, so how was he going to miss? He had tremendous power, and he hit that ball in the Polo Grounds 470 feet. The first day I saw him, I don't know if it was when he first came up, but I think Buck was trying him out and he was hitting the ball all over the place. He was hitting ball after ball into the left field stands.

Lou had a lot of pressure on him. They didn't handle him right. I remember one day he hadn't been playing for a while and Charlie Metro called him over and, of course, Charlie was a different kind of manager. His idea was to keep the players a little unhappy and he tried to be a tough manager. I guess he called it putting the pressure on him. He said, "I'm putting you in, and if you don't come through, you're back on the bench." It's such a game of inches and any little thing that disturbs you can affect the way you play. You have to be able to relax.

We talked quite a bit to Lou and tried to boost his confidence and tell him he had all the tools and it was just a matter of time before he gets to play every day. Everybody knew that.

Favorite time? I kind of remember '61. I hadn't played that much and we were down in Los Angeles one night. I didn't even think I was going to play because Koufax was pitching, and I ended up hitting two home runs and driving in three runs. You were lucky to just make contact off Koufax, let alone hit home runs. I think it impressed someone because I started playing more after that.

Don Cardwell

Don Cardwell had been a Cub for all of two days when he made his first start May 15, 1960. He made quite a first impression. Two days after being acquired from Philadelphia, Cardwell threw a no-hitter in the second game of a Sunday doubleheader against St. Louis at Wrigley Field. "It was a little unusual," Cardwell said about his impressive Cubs debut. The right-hander walked the second batter he faced before retiring 26 in a row in the 4–0 victory. Walt "Moose" Moryn made the final out, catching Joe Cunningham's sinking line drive.

I walked Alex Grammas on a 3–2 pitch in the first inning and it was all downhill then. I played with Alex later on, and I asked him, "How did you take that pitch?" and he said he didn't even see it. I thought it was a good pitch, and the umpire thought it wasn't, and Alex didn't even see it. After the game, everybody who was there was jumping onto the field. I just wanted to get off the field after the game. I had my baseball spikes on and I just didn't want to spike anyone.

George Altman made a good play in right field. And the late Moose Moryn made a great catch on the last out of the ballgame. Cunningham was a good hitter and it was a 3–2 count. He got it about knee-high and halfway down. It was inevitable that Moose was the hero.

I really didn't think about the no-hitter. You don't have to look at the scoreboard. You keep winding up, you don't have to go into the stretch—that's a good sign. Del Rice was catching, and he was a veteran catcher. He came down from Milwaukee at the time. I just stayed with what he said. Lucky it was close. It's not like you're getting pitches eight inches outside like they do today. It's a relief when it's over, when you know what's going on, and you know it's the last out, and you know he made a great catch, and you know it's history.

The next game I started was against Milwaukee, and it was a no-hitter through four and a half innings. After five innings, they called it because of fog. You couldn't see. I had pretty good stuff that night. You never know. But you couldn't see because the fog had rolled in.

I was traded to the Cubs on Friday the 13th. That's a good omen, I guess. My wife had just brought the kids up to Philadelphia and moved into a house, and it was a really big blow to her. It was kind of a hardship on her. Back then, you're on long road trips.

They call you at 7:30 in the morning and tell you to come to the manager's suite. We had just gotten in around 3:30 in the morning. I knew I was going to pitch that day, so I had taken a sleeping pill to sleep. They said, "You're needed in Gene Mauch's suite. You guys have been traded to the Cubs."

I said, "Wait a minute, I can't do that. I'm supposed to pitch today."

And Gene Mauch says, "Not for us."

I've never liked him since then. I guess he had something in mind and they didn't think I fit in with his program. You think about it 40 years later, *c'est la guerre*. We got to Chicago that day, Bouchee and I. Eddie Bouchee was traded with me.

We had pretty good crowds. On September 3, the crowd changes when the kids go back to school. Then you can pick out the people who've been booing you all year, because there's only 3,000 people. "See that guy up there, I know who you are."

What got me traded was the college of coaches. At the end of the year, I went up to Mr. Holland, the general manager, and I said, "Is this going to go on?"

He said, "What? Do you have a problem with it?"

I said, "Yes, sir. I do."

He said, "As long as Mr. Wrigley signs the checks, this is Mr. Wrigley's idea and we'll continue to do this. If you're unhappy with the situation, I'll see what I can do."

In December, it was a three-way trade with the Cubs, Cardinals, and Pirates.

Billy Williams

His swing was pure, powerful, and sweet. Billy Williams made his major league debut August 6, 1959, and became a regular in 1961 when he won Rookie of the Year. He set a National League record for consecutive games played, appearing in 1,117 in a row; he won a batting title in 1972; and he hit 20 or more homers in 14 of his 18 big league seasons. But Williams's journey to the big leagues wasn't as smooth as his swing. The soft-spoken outfielder was probably more influential to the Cubs during the turbulent 1960s than most people know. Elected to baseball's Hall of Fame in 1987, he learned about life and baseball growing up in tiny Whistler, Alabama.

When I left home in 1956, right after I finished high school, I went for two and a half days on a bus to go to Ponca City, Oklahoma. Buck O'Neil said, "An individual will pick you up at the bus station." This guy's name was Mr. Reed, and he picked me up and took me over to his house. In that house was Lou Johnson, Russ Gregg, and a guy by the name of Horace Greenwood from Chicago. They were other black players living in this private home. It made it a little easier.

It seemed like just a great thrill for the people who put us up. I remember the lady used to cook a big meal on Sunday. Her and her husband were the only two people there and we weren't eating there, we were eating at a restaurant. She knew we were going to raid the refrigerator, and she'd make two or three pies on Sunday and leave them there for us.

The following year, all the other players got released or left. That left me the only black on the ballclub, so those times were hard. I think when I went into different cities, people knew that. They would come up to me and offer to take me different places because I was a baseball player. They really tried to cater to me. They knew I was a little homesick kid.

It was a tough time. You go to different cities and they call you all kind of names. Half the time you'd get a base hit, and they were pissed off because you got a base hit, and they'd call you "nigger" or "jigaboo." You hear that—you can't help but hear it. You try to brush all that away from your mind. You don't want anything to take away from what you were doing. Your goal is to play hard and be a good player, and you wash all this shit away. I heard all this until I got to Triple-A.

Every black player who played in the era I played in—you could talk to all of them and they'll have the same story. Fergie [Jenkins] played in Little Rock. They all did this and, of course, they went through the same stuff that I went through—the people, the hatred, the things that they said, the things they tried to do to you to curtail you from what you were trying to do.

There was a case when Buck O'Neil should've got the chance to manage. I think everybody else was thrown out of the game. The only other guy left was the bullpen coach. You had this guy who had been one of the coaches on the coaching staff and he was in a position where he could take over the club, and it didn't happen. I think it kind of made him feel bad and, of course, the black players on the ballclub, they sensed that. It made you uncomfortable. It was a thing you couldn't do anything about.

It's just like an incident that happened in Chicago. I thought Ernie was playing good baseball and I thought he should've been playing first base and he wasn't. I didn't like how that was happening, so I told Jim Enright who was a great friend of Ernie's. Somehow it got back to John Holland, and John Holland called Leo, and Leo called me. Leo said, "I understand you don't like how I'm treating the black ballplayers." It was just Ernie's thing, it wasn't that, because Leo and I got along real well. I just thought Ernie was performing well and he should've been on the field. I told Leo what my opinion was about Ernie, that he was still playing good baseball and I thought he could do a better job than who we put out there. I was reprimanded for that.

I think Ernie wound up going on the field and playing. Ernie was a threat to hit the ball out of the ballpark and a lot of people knew that. He had good hands at first base. I thought he should've been in that position to do that. Just don't cast him out, push him out.

A lot of stuff I did didn't get in the paper. I always was quiet that way. One of the first times we went to Houston, Don Biebel [traveling secretary] had a meeting with all the black players on the ballclub because this was something new down in Houston. He said we could stay at the hotel, but we couldn't go down in the dining room and eat. So I told Don Biebel, "Why don't we go to a black hotel where we have the freedom to move around?"

We wound up going to the team hotel and to the dining room because Don Biebel went in and made a big thing about it because this was how it should be. This wasn't in the paper. I did a lot of things like that, you know, getting with the ballplayers and talking to the guys on the club. I did a lot of things behind closed doors. I think a lot of things should not have been in the paper because you were trying to get something done. I talked to the people. I got to the source. That's what I've always done.

We had a tough time a long time ago. There's no more "take it or leave it." That's what we heard. I think players today are in better condition. They're making a hell of a lot more money than we made, and they want to continue making that money. I just saw where Barry Bonds wants to play until he's 42. That was unheard of when we played because the game was at a fast pace. You had so many great players.

The game hasn't changed. You still got to catch it, you still got to throw it, you still got to hit it. Whether or not you're Tampa Bay, or the New York Yankees, or the Chicago Cubs, you could add one or two players and that's all you need to win a pennant. I think that's changed the game, where you can go out and buy a pennant. I think this has hurt the minor leagues because you get a kid playing Double-A, making progress, playing Triple-A, and he's right on the verge of making the club. He's a left fielder, and all of a sudden they say, "We've got a good ballclub, we don't know if this guy can play left field." He's an unproven guy, so you go out and get a left fielder. Now this kid has been keeping his nose to the grindstone to come up and make the ballclub. Once you get that left fielder, all his hopes are going to be gone. If he doesn't have the right temperament, the right head on his shoulders, he says, "Oh, hell, they're not thinking about me. They just bought a guy."

I think we were caught in that with [Doug] Glanville. We never played Glanville in center field. I knew what he could do because I'd seen him play, but he was always playing left field because we went out and got Brian McRae to play center field. But we wound up trading Glanville and now he's an outstanding player. So this is how the game has changed. With free agency, you can go out and buy a player, you can bring a player in if you're not sure. Who knows? Santo and I might have been hurt that way. We played Double-A and Triple-A. What if the Cubs had been one or two players away and they hadn't known what we could do on a major league level, we could've gotten stymied or went to some other organization.

When I went to $100,000 after 42 home runs, 139 RBI, I went to Mr. Wrigley and said, "You know, Mr. Wrigley, this is what I'd like to get to play this year. If I'm considered one of the top five players in the league, I want to get paid that way." I think I asked for $130,000 or $135,000.

Mr. Wrigley said, "You players are going to price yourselves right out of baseball." That was the money the players made back in the '60s and in the '70s.

The guys who played good, the guys who are playing good at this time in their life, like [Mark] Grace, [Barry] Bonds, [Ken] Griffey, Jr.—these people respect the game of baseball. They know the history of it. You see a lot of guys and they know who walked on that field, who played good baseball, and that's what keeps them going. That's baseball.

I often tell them, your playing career goes by so fast. Give all you've got while you're on the field. Don't walk in the clubhouse and say if I coulda, woulda, shoulda. Try to leave it all out on the field. You're only out there three and a half to four hours. Make sure it's all done.

Lou Brock

How could the Cubs let Lou Brock go? Brock made his major league debut in a Cubs uniform on September 10, 1961, and played two full seasons before he became part of what is unofficially dubbed the worst trade in baseball history. On June 15, 1964, Brock, Jack Spring, and Paul Toth were dealt to St. Louis for one-time 21-game winner Ernie Broglio, Bobby Shantz, and Doug Clemens. Brock played for the Cardinals until 1979, became one of the game's greatest base stealers, and was eventually elected to the Hall of Fame in 1985. But, as a young Cub, he was just trying to get his footing in the game.

Buck O'Neil was the first black coach in major league baseball. In fact, Buck O'Neil signed me. He came to the big leagues and I roomed with Buck for about a year. I think he was my roommate longer than anybody, and I had George Altman for a short while, and Billy Williams, and Ernie Banks. My real roommate was Buck O'Neil, and those guys would kid me all the time that I was the only person in the big leagues who had his own coach.

I knew Buck from college days. He's the one who, quote, discovered me in college. Buck's a fine manager, a fine person. I named one of my kids after Buck and the kid is in Stanford right now in his third year, so the name of Buck O'Neil will live on.

I was a player with two left feet learning my way around in baseball when I was with the Cubs. I don't think you really have a grasp or you're grounded or rooted in your confidence or experience, so things can be a little hectic. Of course, I probably fit the mold of 99 percent of the players who come along like that.

The Cubs were pretty good, just like all ballplayers. I think all ballclubs are pretty good at having somebody on the club who can talk to you and instill some confidence in you at the same time. But even some of the great players who are in the game, they can become preoccupied with their own experiences or their own set of circumstances and may not have a lot of time to input a lot of things to you. On a ballclub like the Cubs back in the '60s, things were unsettled a bit because I was there with the 14-man coaching staff. That was a tough thing to get used to, so there wasn't a lot of time for guys to bring a young player along, because they had to deal with those kind of circumstances as well.

I only saw one or two of the veteran players able to handle that. Ernie Banks certainly was one of them; George Altman did a good job of it; but everybody else was affected—even Ron Santo was affected by it. There were a lot of changes being made at the time as well, so you had a lot of young players like myself, and Danny Murphy, and Billy Ott, and Billy Cowan—some of the guys who were coming along at that time—who needed to be melded into this Cub organization and try to become grounded and rooted. It was very difficult when you've got 14 people to answer to.

I think they had a manual called "The Cub Way," so you could go to that to get a pretty good idea of what you were supposed to be doing. I read it as best I knew how, but when you get out on the field in competition, you better know how to play baseball. We got a big laugh out of that, but it wasn't funny at the time.

There's something called a "glimpse." You hear that expression, "There's a glimpse of greatness" and it comes once in a while. The question becomes, over a period of time, will that glimpse become a reality, or is that it as we see it? Sometimes the organization, particularly in my case, takes the position of a glimpse. Maybe it's there, but it will never come together in his career. The other part of that is people gamble that it will come together, that you will reach some consistency with each glimpse. So I had a lot of great glimpses with the Cubs. There were days I was outstanding, there were days that I looked like I never saw a baseball. So the question is, where is the common denominator? Where is the consistency in this guy? It was my third year when I got traded, so consequently the glimpse was still there, but the performance wasn't.

In my particular case, I was like Keith Hernandez, J. D. Drew. Wherever we have played prior to coming to the big leagues, we've already batted .300. So you get to the big leagues and you're batting less than .300, and you think there's a problem with you, not necessarily the league, and you have a hard time overcoming that. I was no different. I thought, if I'm not hitting .300, I'm not playing up to my potential. Maybe these guys are greater than I thought they were. Hopefully I can hang on to get one year or another year in. Then, lo and behold, they said, "Your contract has been transferred."

Well, you knew it was going to come because you're already thinking that you're playing below the standards in the league, and you'd been a .300 hitter all your life so you don't know what failure is. Hitting .240, .260 to me was a failure. That's what I hit my first year, .263. That was a failure. I was looking for how you improve on that, so when the call came that I was traded—in fact I didn't get traded, they just said, "Your contract has been transferred"—that had no meaning. Where? Transferred? Where? Waxahatchee? Walla Walla? Where am I going?

Then they finally said, "You've been transferred to the St. Louis Cardinals."

My initial reaction was, "What do they want with me?"

But it also raises your stock in your confidence. It's headed to another level simply because they say, "We're getting Ernie Broglio and it's a deal we had to make" et cetera. Broglio—that's an outstanding pitcher. You stick your chest out. "Hey, listen, I got traded for Ernie Broglio. Did you hear that?" My stock went up.

Most people don't realize that when I got traded from the Cubs I had a nine-game hitting streak, and I was hitting .450 in that streak, so I was already hot. But my average was so low nobody saw that, not even the Cubs. So when I got to St. Louis, there was a continuation of that. It's part of that glimpse that I was telling you about. That nine-game glimpse looked great. Could it last? That particular glimpse lasted for the next 16 years, 17 years. Perhaps when you turn corners, sometimes an organization may look at your weakness so long they don't see progress. I think that's what happened to the Cubs in my case. But on the other hand, the Cubs had a chance to get a 21-game winner and the year before we had lost something like 20, 25 one-run games. Cut that in half and you're in the hunt. Broglio was the kind of pitcher capable of winning half of them. So when I got traded, I was just happy to still be in the big leagues because my contract was transferred.

Not too many people came out to cover that trade. I remember the *Chicago American* sending out a youngster to cover the trade and he did a tongue-in-cheek story. The content led to the headline, "The Cubs Have Just Pulled Off the Greatest Steal Since the Brinks Robbery." We know that young reporter today as Brent Musburger. Little did he know. I proved him wrong.

The worst trade ever? I have a hard time with that, although it sounds nice and makes you chuckle. Somehow people believe that. They talk about Babe Ruth and Babe Ruth being the worst purchase, and then they say I was part of the worst trade. I think it's only because it has the word "Cubs" attached to it. It's the Cub factor.

Ernie Broglio

Ernie Broglio led the National League with 21 wins in 1960 and won 18 games in 1963 with St. Louis. But whenever the right-handed pitcher's name is mentioned, he is always on the short end of what is considered the most lopsided Cubs trade ever. On June 15, 1964, Broglio was dealt to Chicago in a six-player swap that included a light-hitting outfielder named Lou Brock. The rest is history. Brock helped the Cardinals win the World Series that year and went on to a Hall of Fame career, while Broglio won only seven games over three seasons with the Cubs. Broglio didn't have a physical before the trade was made. He should have. He now teaches youngsters aged 9 to 18 at a baseball school in San Jose, California, about the intricacies of pitching. He isn't bothered by his infamy.

It's funny that they remember the trade, but they don't remember that I won 18 games the year before. That doesn't bother me because we were professional, and it was the media that proceeded in making it the "worst trade" and everything.

Lou was not a .300 hitter at the time. I came up with an 18-win year, and we were both at the bottom of the league, and I had had a real good career against the Cubs. I don't think I had to do anything to justify the trade. You always put pressure on yourself to make yourself look good. The pressure for me came after the operation. Now, I've got pressure on myself to keep myself in the big leagues.

In those days, being traded was accepted. It was disheartening because you do form a camaraderie with the ballplayers. You spend five years with one of the greatest ballplayers, Stan Musial, and you feel a little disappointed about leaving. Sometimes you wish you could end up with the ballclub that gave you a chance to stay in the big leagues. I was disappointed, sure. But I went to a ballclub with some great ballplayers on it. The only thing I disliked was day baseball. The last time I played day baseball was in high school, and once I signed, everything was night baseball. I just had a tough time adjusting to day baseball.

I thought if Leo could've stayed with me, he was the type of manager I needed to play for. He was mean enough to get something out of me. I told him that after many years. I told him if he would've stayed with me, I think I could've really done some justice for him.

Leo was all over Randy Hundley. One time, Leo got so mad at Randy that he threw a towel up and smashed his hand in the dugout. We were all sitting there, and we had to put our hands over our faces to keep from laughing so hard. Randy had a tough time throwing the ball back to the pitcher sometimes. He could never get the ball high enough or sometimes the pitcher had to jump off the mound to get it. Randy was never a curser either. He never swore. Leo would say, "At least say 'sh——' something or 'goddamn.'"

I had tendinitis in my shoulder when I was with the Cardinals. Every other start, I had to have a cortisone shot. I didn't know anything about it, they just stuck a needle in me. The final one they stuck in me was the big one and that was as close as I came to passing out. I won 20, came back, and had shoulder problems.

The operation I had on my elbow, if I was playing nowadays, I'd be out of here. I had an operation in November 1964 and I was in spring training in February. They transferred a ligament from one area of my elbow to the area where it belonged. Plus bone chips had formed around it. I was in the hospital in November, right around Thanksgiving, and two and a half months later I was in spring training.

You didn't think about the pain. It was a situation where you didn't want to sit out. They rehabbed me a little bit longer. I still was in spring training and today, you're out a year if you have any type of elbow surgery. If they'd had the Tommy John operation in those days, I probably would've had that instead of what they did. I was a few years ahead of that.

I was pretty secretive. The shoulder problem was tendinitis and everybody goes through that. I think this thing with my elbow was there for a long time. All of a sudden, after innings pitched and breaking balls, this thing started tearing.

The only way people know about injuries now is that they put people on the disabled list. I'm sure there are ballplayers now who play hurt. Heck, I've seen guys in the clubhouse where they drew water out of their knee and they'd go out and play. Take Ron Santo. When he got hit in the head, his eye was closed and red, and two days later, he was out there playing.

I think you had that in your blood, not so much fear of losing your job, but that you were at the top and you wanted to play no matter what. In those days, when you fought for a contract, you had to really fight. The more games you played, the more games you won, the more innings you pitched, the more money you got.

They talk about collusion now. The year I won 21 games, my second year, they told me I should ask for a $1,000-a-game raise. I said fine, so when they sent me the contract, they sent me a $5,000 raise. So I sent it back and said this wasn't what I wanted. I was only making $7,500 at the time. They sent back a counteroffer that was the same thing. Their final word to me—I had missed a week of spring training—was, "We don't need you, you need us."

I said, "Boy, oh boy, you got that right. I've got four children and a brand new house." I left San Jose on a Sunday morning at 7:00 and I was in St. Petersburg Wednesday morning. Drove straight through without stopping. I signed a contract, and 40 minutes later I was taking batting practice. That was the difference. You were hungry. You wanted to continue.

I'm still remembered. The trade's brought up all the time. The bad thing about it, I went from a case of Budweiser to a pack of Wrigley's spearmint gum. That's what really upset me. And a World Series ring. That was disappointing. If it wasn't for Lou, they would've never won a pennant that year. He went from .230

to hitting over .300. What he did ignited that whole baseball team. Sometimes a trade is good. It turned out to be the greatest thing to happen to Lou. It backfired with the Cubs. If I hadn't been hurt, I think it would've been a different story.

That's one thing that the Cardinals organization did, they made you feel comfortable. They absolutely made you feel at home. In Chicago, it was more the ballplayers who made you feel at home and not the front office. The whole organization in St. Louis made you feel at home. I was three years with the Cubs and never met Mr. Wrigley. I was five years with the Cardinals and every spring met Mr. [August] Busch.

Glenn Beckert

Second baseman Glenn Beckert totaled 22 home runs in nine seasons with the Cubs, so it wasn't his powerful swing that kept him in the lineup from 1965 to 1973. Beckert did the little things and was one of manager Leo Durocher's favorites. Beckert and shortstop Don Kessinger complemented each other, even if they were opposites. Rheumatoid arthritis hampered Beckert during his final three seasons. "Back then, you thought baseball was going to last forever," he says. The game lives on in his memories.

I put the ball in play. I didn't have the ability to hit home runs, and I liked the lifestyle of the major leagues. I think I fit in good with the team because I had Billy Williams, and Santo, and Ernie Banks. My job was to move the runner along. I was very fortunate. We had some good ballplayers.

Everything is based on home runs now. I think if guys could hit .300 and develop a style of moving runners along, they'd be more valuable. Everybody is home run conscious now. Everybody always looks at the home run hitters—the McGwires, the Sosas, guys like that. A lot of guys could make themselves better ballplayers by learning more about the game.

Leo helped me, Alvin Dark, guys like that helped me. A fellow in Pittsburgh who had a lot of power, Dick Groat, their shortstop, he was more of a line-drive, singles-type hitter. I tried to follow his pattern. My first year, I was swinging from my heels and hit .239. I realized back in those days, you hit .239, you don't stick around too long. I developed it. I said, "Hey, I've got to do something if I'm going to stay here." Look, if you strike out 150 times a year, nothing happens. So if a guy is hitting .260 and he's striking out 160, 170 times a year, he's not helping out the team. You have to analyze what your ability is and stay within it. I could've hit 10, 15 home runs a year, but what could that have done if I'd hit .220? You have to realize what your position is on the team and what's expected of you.

I think when we played there was a lot more team concept. There was no free agency and guys stuck together. You knew who was on the Pittsburgh Pirates, St. Louis. Now, one or two guys stay there five or seven years. I think that's one of the good points of the game when I played. I think that's why they remember our team, the '69 Cubs. The nucleus was together nine years. There were seven, eight of us. It seems like yesterday. Just to be remembered for not winning is amazing. It's the Cub charisma or whatever. I've been very fortunate. We were able to set up great friendships, not only with the players, but the wives. As I look back, it's a great treasure.

If we'd won in '69, we would've won in '70 and '71. I think '70 was the best team I ever played for. We picked up Joe Pepitone and Rick Monday, but we just couldn't break through.

Kess and I, we're somewhat different personalities. Kess is laid back and I'm charging at all times. We had to do something right, we were together all that time. After a while it just became instinct. I knew what his limitations were, and he knew what mine were. I knew where his throw was going to be nine out of ten times. I saw the other side of it when I went to San Diego. They had a Latin player, Hernandez, and he didn't speak English and I didn't speak Spanish. Shortstop, second, center field were the nucleus. I said, "Man, oh man, do I appreciate Kess now." I wish I had taken Spanish in school.

My favorite Cubs moment, the all-time game—and I probably had better stats in certain games—but my parents were from an agricultural background from western Pennsylvania. We were playing Pittsburgh at Wrigley Field and they weren't much for traveling. They got the box seats in the front row. In the game in the ninth inning, Kess got a hit and I think I got the key hit, first and third, nobody out, and after Billy Williams knocked in the winning run or whatever, I went over to my parents, and my dad and mother had tears in their eyes. You could see the pride. You could just see their happiness radiating from them. Being from Pittsburgh, beating them. It was just nice.

My dad had to work, my mother took care of the house. It's not like the mobile society that we live in today. It was a little more laid back then. I certainly appreciate being raised at that time. Life wasn't as fast back then.

Leo, I don't know. He just liked me. It started when it was first announced that he was coming and I had a year in. I was Chicago rookie of the year—why, I don't know. I guess I was the only pick. They had a dinner, I think it was at the Palmer House. They had Koufax there and Willie Mays. I looked around the dais, and I said, "There aren't too many .239 hitters here, but there's Mr. Durocher." And we hit it off.

Somehow I always got my uniform dirty diving for a ball, and looking back I think I reminded him of him. I really appreciated Leo. He was very kind to me. Leo had a way. He liked Randy. Randy had this laid-back, southern Virginia style. Leo would call the pitches and he used to drive Randy crazy. But he didn't get rid of him. He caught every game. Maybe he shouldn't have. Back then, he was scared. There were three, four guys behind you. You're on a one-year contract.

I wouldn't trade it for anything. I got to meet a lot of wonderful people. I belong to one of the nicest fraternities, playing in the major leagues. I'm not boasting or anything, but you talk and people say, "You played in the big leagues?" It's good for an old guy's ego.

Leo was one who liked to have center stage. The Hollywood thing, Frank Sinatra. He liked to be No. 1. I think he wanted to eliminate the old-school thought, that old country club attitude that was with the Cubs. "Country club" means you go and play and you're never going to win anything. Nothing against Ernie personally, but when Leo looked at Ernie, it was the old country club attitude. I don't think they really got along. But how can you not get along with Ernie Banks? I think Leo tolerated Ernie because he was producing. If you're producing, personalities don't enter into it.

Leo liked veteran players. I don't know how it developed, but Kess and I hit it off real good with him. Leo wasn't much for patience when it came to pitching. Leo's theory was when you got to the major leagues, you were ready to pitch. But you've got to give the man credit. Not only did he like me, but he changed the attitude and created interest. When you're in the entertainment business, that's what it's all about.

Ron Santo

He is the third baseman all other Chicago Cubs third basemen are com-
pared to. Ron Santo played for the Cubs from 1960 to 1973 and spent
one apathetic season with the White Sox in 1974. A nine-time All-Star,
he won five Gold Gloves and hit 342 home runs in 15 seasons. His
favorite year was the heartbreaking 1969 season when the Cubs were in
first place until late September and finished second in the National
League East with a 92–70 record. Even though he doesn't wear a uni-
form to the broadcast booth as an analyst for WGN radio, Santo still
bleeds Cubs blue. You can hear it in his voice.

I opened in Pittsburgh. I'd never been to a big league park in my
life. We had a nine-game losing streak. It was June 26. Lou
Boudreau was the manager. He put me in there. I went 4 for 7, I
drove in five runs. We win a doubleheader, and then we come
into Wrigley Field.

When I first went to Wrigley Field, I'll never forget it. I'll
never forget leaving the clubhouse in the left field corner and
walking with Ernie Banks. In those days, when you were a
rookie, your teammates wouldn't talk to you, but Ernie talked to
me. We're going out and he said, "What's this feel like?"

I said, "Ernie, I can't believe it."

I walked on the field and there was an atmosphere. There's
nothing like it. The stands were empty. It was so beautiful. It was
like playing in my backyard. It didn't feel like, "Jeez, I'm over-
whelmed." It felt like, "This is baseball."

To me, '69 was the greatest year I've ever spent in Chicago. We all had this feeling in spring training. Leo Durocher had taken over in '66, and he said, "We're not an eighth-place team." We finished tenth. The next year, we finished third. Then third again. And then you could see it all coming together—Kessinger, Beckert, and the pitching staff. We didn't talk about it, but in '69, everybody had that feeling that this was it. We started off and Willie Smith hit that home run and that was magical. That year was special up until September of that game against the Pirates, when [Willie] Stargell hit the home run in the ninth.

We had just come back from the West Coast and we were 2–7. The Mets had won and were within three games of us. It was the first game home. Phil Regan on the mound, 1–0 ballgame, and Willie Stargell hits a 1–2 pitch out of the ballpark against a 30-mile-an-hour wind. I dropped my head and said, "What's going to happen now?" We lost that game. We didn't talk about it. We talked about the tough luck we had on the coast. But that was the only time that whole year we ever felt things were changing. Up until then, it didn't matter who we played or how far we were behind, we were going to win the ballgame.

In early June in '69, the Cardinals and the Pirates were the teams. The Mets were right there, but nobody was worried about the Mets. We were one game ahead and we were playing Montreal in a doubleheader. The Cardinals were playing that day, and if we'd lost both games, we would've been tied for first place. We lost the first game. In the second, we're down two runs. We have runners at first and second, and Jim Hickman's the hitter. Two outs, bottom of the ninth. He hits a home run. I go to home plate and I crown him on the head—he keeps talking about how he got a headache from me pounding him so bad. When that game was over, I ran down to the clubhouse and I went up in the air and clicked my heels once. I didn't know I did it. It just happened.

I get home, and I always watch WGN-TV because you can see the highlights. I was looking for Hickman's home run. I'm sitting down and the news comes on, and the first thing they showed was me running down. The newscasters are saying, "There's Ron Santo clicking his heels after a win against Montreal."

The next day, I come to the ballpark and Durocher calls a meeting. He said, "Ron, do you think you could click your heels again?"

I said, "I don't know Skip. I didn't even know I did it."

He said, "The way things are going for us, why don't we make that the victory kick at home?"

OK, so we win the next day and I'm going down to the clubhouse and, for some reason, the fans are not leaving the ballpark. They're waiting. I click my heels three times, and I spike myself the last time—I'll never forget that. And that was our victory kick.

I would never do it on the road, and I'd only do it if we won at home. We were winning so much. And all of a sudden, I started to get knocked down a lot. I put it together. I wasn't showing up the pitcher. The game was over. I didn't click my heels when I hit a home run.

Then Tim McCarver, who was catcher for the Cardinals, he calls me. He was a friend of mine. He said, "I'll meet you at the corner." We couldn't fraternize, see. He said, "Ron, I just want you to know our pitchers aren't happy about you clicking your heels."

All I said to him was, "Timmy, when I go across those white lines, nobody is my friend. You just let them know I don't care."

I loved Leo. I loved him. But we clashed. The only way I can explain this is I'm a very friendly guy. Off the field, I love people. On the field, I'm a different guy. And that's the way Durocher was. Durocher was a great guy off the field. He was a lot of fun.

He was a players' manager. On the field, he was a prick. He was tough. And he hurt you any way he could. We clashed a lot. There was a lot of stuff he did that I didn't like. But there was a lot of stuff he did that I liked. He got the best out of the players. I look at a guy like Jim Leyland. I look at Tony La Russa. They have a way about them to get the best out of players who don't have all the talent in the world.

Leo didn't have to kick me in the ass, but there was one time when I was in a slump. It was June and I'm still hitting over .300 and leading the club in RBI and I'm hitting fourth in the lineup. I was the captain. I would take the lineup card out to the umpires. Usually Leo would walk over and give me the card and say, "How's so-and-so doing?" He'd always confide in me. He always had a comment. On this particular day, he comes over, hands me the card, and walks away. I put the card in my pocket and go out to loosen up. Billy Williams came over to me. Now we never changed the lineup. Billy says, "Any changes in the lineup?" I take it out, and I'm hitting seventh. I look at this, and I'm pissed.

Leo used to stand behind the cage and watch hitting. Every day, arms crossed, watch hitting, and then he'd walk away. So, he's back there. It's my turn to hit and because I'm hitting seventh, I'm in the third group. And I'm pissed. I get up there and take ten swings; the next time, five swings; the next time, three; and another three. After the last turn, I turned and looked right at him, and I threw the bat at the cage and I walked out of the cage.

The game starts and I go 4 for 4, two home runs, and drove in five runs. What did he do? He got me on track. He won that battle. I didn't realize it. He got me out of the slump.

You don't know how tough it was to leave the Chicago Cubs. When general manager John Holland called me, my first wife was sick with salmonella poisoning. I had taken her to the hospital in the middle of the night. The next morning, John calls me and he says, "Ron, we've got a chance. You know we're moving players.

This is the toughest thing I've ever had to do. You're a 5-and-10 player and you have a right to turn it down, but we have a chance to get three pitchers from the California Angels and they want you bad. They're willing to give you a two-year deal, unbelievable money."

I said, "John, you called me at a bad time. My wife is in the hospital, and I don't have time to talk about it or even discuss it. Call me in a week."

I hung up the phone and I had tears. I didn't cry, I just had tears.

A week later, he calls me. I said, "John, I'm not going to move my family to California." I was making over $100,000, and I was making as much money off the field. I still felt I had a couple years left and I wanted to be a Cub.

Then he really hurt me and said, "Where do you want to go?"

I had to hang up the phone. I bawled because I knew that was it. I called him back and said, "I'm going to retire. I'm not going anywhere."

The Cubs were getting Bill Madlock. Then Bill Wrigley, Jr., called and said, "Ron, we don't want you to retire. We want you to come back to the Cubs as a player and a coach."

I said, "I can't do that." I still had a lot of baseball left in me.

Then I got a call from White Sox manager Chuck Tanner, and I was staying in Chicago. To be honest, when that happened, I lost my desire and love for the game. I hit .300 that last year with the Cubs, I had 25 home runs or whatever. But I lost my enthusiasm. Even though I was happy to stay in Chicago, it wasn't the same.

Tanner had told me, "You're going to play third, you'll play left, you'll play first. You're not ready for DH'ing." I had a two-year, no-cut contract, making about $130,000 a year. I was in Florida, wearing that White Sox uniform and I can't believe it. Tanner comes over and puts his arm around me and said, "It's good to have you. We know what you can do. You know what I'd like you to do? Could you stay away from third base?"

When he told me that, I realized right then and there that this would be my last year. Normally, I carry my feelings on my sleeve. I said to him, "How can you tell me that when this has been my life?" I felt that Chicago was Chicago, and that's why I chose the White Sox. But in all honesty, I wish I had just shut it down right then.

Don Kessinger

Leo Durocher is often credited with persuading Don Kessinger to become a switch-hitter. Well, that's not exactly true. The slender shortstop can explain what really happened and pays homage to his Cubs teammates. Kessinger played for the Cubs from 1964 to 1975, and was part of a solid defensive infield that included second baseman Glenn Beckert, third baseman Ron Santo, and first baseman Ernie Banks.

Let me say this so it doesn't sound like I'm calling Leo a liar or something, which I'm not. I have tremendous respect for what Leo Durocher did as a baseball person. I appreciate that Leo Durocher put me in the lineup to play every day.

The way the switch-hitting came about was I came up the end of 1964, and 1965 was my first year and I really, really struggled. I'd hit good in college; I'd hit good in Double-A. I came to the big leagues and hit .201 that year. Toward the end of that year, 1965, there were a couple weeks left in the season, and I said to Alvin Dark, who was one of our coaches, "Alvin, I believe I can switch-hit."

He said, "Have you ever done it?"

I said, "No."

He said, "What makes you think you can switch-hit?"

I said, "I don't know, I just think I can switch-hit."

He said, "Well, if you could, it would be a tremendous boost to your career, because the way you play defense you can play in the big leagues for a long time. But they'll always be looking for the guy who can play defense like you do and hit .250, .260, .270. If you do that, they quit looking. Here's what I suggest you do: I suggest you go home in the off-season and you get in the gym with a tennis ball. You have somebody throw to you really hard, because the first thing you have to find out is if you can get away from the ball. Because it's different."

And I did that.

So I came back the next spring. The Cubs had made a change that winter and hired Leo. When I got to spring training that next year, we had an early camp for some of us in Escondido, California. Lou Klein was running the early camp. I said, "Lou, I've worked on switch-hitting during the off-season, and I'd like to work on switch-hitting."

He said, "I need to ask Leo about it."

I said, OK, that's fine.

I didn't hear anything about it for a couple of weeks. Lou Klein came back to me and said, "They just want you to keep hitting right-handed and work on hitting the ball to the opposite field."

I said OK, so I did. We went on through spring training and opened the season, and I was hitting my usual .230 or whatever.

In late May of 1966, we were taking batting practice one day in Wrigley Field before a game and Leo walked up to me at the batting cage and his quote was, "I just heard yesterday that you wanted to switch-hit this spring."

And I said, "Well, yeah, I did." So I got in there and I hit the ball.

And he said, in Leo's way of saying things, "You swing better that way than you do right-handed."

I said, "Thanks. Thanks a lot." I'd been working 20 years hitting right-handed.

He said, "You should take batting practice a few days and let's see what happens."

I took batting practice really only two days batting left-handed, and Leo called me down in the middle of the game—it was one of those rare games in 1966 when we were ahead—and he said, "This would be a good time for you to try to hit left-handed."

I said, "Good night, I've only done it two days." But I hit left-handed the rest of my life, and that was it.

Let me give Leo credit for something. I was hitting about .230, I went right down to about .190 [batting left-handed]. I remember walking off the field one day to that old dressing room back down in the corner, and as we're walking down the field, I said, "Skip, why don't we wait until next year to work on this."

He said, "No, absolutely not. Absolutely not. I want you to keep hitting that way because that's going to help your career."

So I've got to give him lots of credit for that. He stayed right with me and helped me with that. That's exactly the way the deal happened.

Let me tell you truly, that group of guys—I was so fortunate to come to the Cubs at a time when we had such great role models. I was a young guy. Beck and I came up the same year. We had guys like Ernie Banks, and Billy Williams, and Ron Santo, and George Altman. These were great guys. Not just good players, but great guys. It was great for us to be around a group like that. Beck and I used to go out early, especially when Alvin Dark was the coach that first year. We used to go out 20 minutes before other people to take ground balls and work on double plays; so yeah, we did become close, and I think we're good friends today. That whole group of guys were good friends. That's the thing that people don't understand. That was the great thing about that group that stayed together for so many years. We really cared about each other. There was a unique relationship between the players and between the players and the fans with that group of guys that in all my 16 years we were never able to emulate. It was really a unique deal.

We were bad in 1965 and worse in 1966 and Leo took over and said, "I guarantee this is not an eighth-place ballclub." He was right, because we finished tenth. We were bad. But then in 1967 we went from tenth to third. In June or July of that summer, we won a ballgame that put us in first place, and from that moment on there was this deal with this group of people and the fans. Nineteen sixty-eight was better. We were really good and we finished third again but we were good, and '69 was just a magical year that didn't end right. I don't know how it could've been more wild than having won it.

Bob Kennedy

When Bob Kennedy took over as the Cubs head coach in 1963, it brought an end to the rotation element of the infamous college of coaches. He was the manager without the title. The Cubs went 82–80 in Kennedy's first season, topping .500 for the first time in 17 years. The 1964 season was marred by the death of talented second baseman Ken Hubbs, who was killed in an airplane crash. Kennedy says the team never recovered from the tragedy. Kennedy managed for two months in '65 before departing, but he returned to the Cubs from 1977 to 1981 as the general manager. Among the players he signed was controversial slugger Dave Kingman.

Pitching is the main thing with most clubs, and pitching in Wrigley Field has been the history of success. But you're looking at history. Do you know the first time the Cubs won a World Series? The first one was in August 1876, and Custer was getting beat in the Little Big Horn. That's a fact. They only played 62 games in those days.

One of the things that hurt the Cubs for years was that at one point Mr. Wrigley—and I think it was just before I got there in '63, a year or two before that—he didn't draft anybody for two or three years. He just didn't do it. He recommended that it not be done. If you're building a farm system, it really takes some time.

I came after the college of coaches. I wouldn't take the job that way. In '62, I was managing in Salt Lake. I wasn't going to take the job. Herman Franks was running the Salt Lake team, and he said, "Bob, you've got a chance to manage in the big leagues, you've got to take it."

I think the reason Mr. Wrigley did the college of coaches was that he was tired of firing managers. Here's a manager one year who had a good year, but then he didn't do well the next year. Mr. Wrigley was trying to figure out some way to keep from firing managers. At least he tried it.

We got along pretty good. I was with Phil Wrigley when his mother and dad both died. I enjoyed my time there. The odd part about it was here's a South Sider who played with the White Sox and ended up managing on the North Side. I played almost ten years with the White Sox, then spent almost seven or eight years on the North Side.

I don't think the money was there. The club was privately owned. It was the Wrigley family, not the company. That's when agents started. A lot of money was being spent, more money than usual. It almost was getting to the point where a team had to be company owned.

Herman was managing in '78 or '79, and we didn't lose a series from May to September. In one week, we had everybody and his brother get hurt. Pitching is a paramount issue there. That 368 in the alleys is tough. Not only is it short, but a lot of balls hit into that area that the center fielder and right fielder could get, they have to back up because of the wall. And when the wind blows out there, it really blows.

The thing that hurt us with the Cubs was Kenny Hubbs. He was right in the middle of the field and he was an outstanding ballplayer. You don't replace those players. Banks for years carried everything there, then Billy Williams came along, and Santo. [Don] Kessinger came in a little later and [Glenn] Beckert. They didn't come together, they came at different points. There's no question—you have to have super pitching. You have to have good pitching.

Kingman was a good guy, contrary to what people say. He was always in shape and always on time. He'll be the only one who hit over 400 home runs who won't get into the Hall of Fame. I have a theory on that, that some players who do so good get all the attention, and then they duck it because they don't want that pressure. As far as a young fellow and being a prospect, he had more talent than anybody. He could run, he had a good arm, he could hit. He just couldn't stand the attention.

When I was signing him, Mr. Wrigley was at the table and I think Kingman's agent was there. Kingman said, "What would you give me if I broke the RBI record?"

I said, "I'll give you $100,000."

I thought Mr. Wrigley was going to jump off the chair. He said, "What is it?"

I said, "It's 190, set by a Cub, Hack Wilson."

There were some things I wish I could've done. There's no question there were some times I wish I had kept my mouth shut, I would've been a lot better off. That's always going to be. I really enjoyed it and was very thankful. I've been really lucky that I've had all the jobs I've had. The only three I haven't had in baseball are owner, trainer, and umpire.

Randy Hundley

So, how difficult was it to catch 100-plus games in the summer heat? Randy Hundley knows. He was the only man to catch 150 games three consecutive seasons with the Cubs. Sometimes it was even more difficult for Hundley to deal with Cubs manager Leo Durocher than extra innings behind home plate. Hundley's son Todd has also strapped on the so-called tools of ignorance in the big leagues. Many have said the Cubs will never win as long as they play the majority of their games in the daytime. How tough was it?

The thing of it is, when you're young, you don't pay any attention to that stuff. It was a lot more exhausting than I realized it was. I think the bad thing about the day games is you're tired, you didn't get a good night's sleep, you still got to get up and get with it. You can't sleep in. You have this schedule that you have to meet and you've got to go do it. I can recall times when I would literally be sick and go to the ballpark.

One time I got dehydrated and couldn't wake up in the morning. My parents were visiting at the time, so I had to let my dad drive me to the ballpark. I got to the park, and I just couldn't put one foot in front of the other. I guess the point I'm making is that if it were a night game, I could've gotten my rest. Because it was a day game, I didn't recover from it. I think I tried to play that day. The next day, we went on a road trip to Cincinnati and I was still dehydrated. I didn't know what the heck was happening. The only thing I knew was to keep on going. Every time I'd sit down I'd go to sleep. I finally got up enough energy to get to the ballpark, and they looked at me and said something's wrong. They took me to the airport and sent me back to Chicago and found out I was dehydrated, and I missed a few days because of that.

I loved playing day ball. I felt you could see the ball a lot better. I just didn't like hitting under the lights. It was a major adjustment for me. When you play night games, you finish up, you get to the hotel at midnight, it takes you two, three hours to unwind, and it's the middle of the night when you go to bed. You're not on a regular routine.

My first year, Leo drove me nuts. I thought, if this is major league baseball, I don't want it, I don't need it, take this job and shove it. My second year, he turned it over to me and said, "Randy, you're my manager on the field and whatever you say goes." I think he wanted to train me to his way of playing the game, and he felt that I was doing what he wanted me to do.

The first year, he'd say, "You dumb, no-good so-and-so, how can you call for that pitch?" Well, the guy just threw the pitch down the middle of the plate and the guy hit it nine miles. It was his way of getting to the pitcher going through me. Players used to look at me and cross their eyes and say, "How do you take that?" I don't know how I take it.

I loved him. Leo gave me an opportunity to play. You can't ask for any more than that. I think he liked me. In the long run, I think he liked me a lot and I was appreciated a lot.

My sense in '69 was that we didn't have enough pitching. I think, in retrospect—at the time we don't know anything about it—but I think Leo could've used his bench a little better. I think he could've used Paul Popovich at all the infield positions a little more to give all the guys a little break. He probably could've put somebody behind the plate for me a couple times. In '69, I caught 155, 154 games. That's a lot of ballgames. They're not games I went in to substitute for. They were complete ballgames.

People, especially Cubs fans, don't realize how well the Mets played. They were unbeatable. I kept looking up and thinking they haven't been in a slump yet, they're going to get in a slump, and that's when we'll blow right past them. Then they go in and beat Atlanta in the play-offs. And who would've thought they'd beat Baltimore?

They had outstanding pitching. Pitching is what failed us in the long run. I've read about guys going in slumps and what not. You still win ballgames with pitching. If you don't give up runs, you don't have to hit very much. And we wore Phil Regan out. It got to the point where his arm was about to fall off. I'm a firm believer in fate. It just wasn't meant to be.

You get along with certain pitchers in different ways. Bill Hands and I were traded from the Giants to the Cubs. We had some tough times in the Giants organization. He was kind of a high-strung, hard-headed mother and so was I, and we used to do battle quite a bit. Over the year, I could look at him and I could see in his eyes he didn't want that pitch. I'd say, "OK, here try this one, pal." He'd start his windup and he'd go right at it.

We played a game at Wrigley Field one day and Bill Hands was pitching and Leo came to me before the game and said, "Now, Randy, don't tell Foggie, but I'm going to call the pitches today." We were playing on national TV. I said, OK. So, every pitch I looked in the dugout. I'd see him standing out there shaking off, and I'd give him the sign three times. They took Bill Hands out in the fifth inning. They took me out in the sixth inning. I had two pop-ups above my head that I missed. I go into the locker room and Bill Hands is pacing up and down. He said, "Roomie, that's the worst blankety-blank game you ever called in your life."

I listened to him for 15 minutes. I finally said, "Roomie, I didn't call any of those pitches."

He said, "Thank God. I thought you were losing your mind."

Todd had it on at a mighty young age. I don't think he knew I was a player. I'll never forget coming off a road trip in Cincinnati. It was like his fourth or fifth birthday, and my wife had signed him up for T-ball. I said, "What position did he sign up for?"

She said, "He wants to be a catcher."

I was on the MacGregor staff and brought this whole MacGregor catching stuff to him for his birthday, and he's been a catcher ever since. I don't think he knew I was a ballplayer.

He knew he wanted to be a ballplayer when he was two. He constantly had a ball and glove in his hand. I was that way as a kid myself. My blood cells and Todd's blood cells have baseball written all over them.

Todd kept saying he wanted to be a ballplayer. OK, if you want to be a ballplayer, you've got to work. I don't think he realized how much work it was going to take. My other son wanted to be a pilot, and I said, "OK, great, let's work on it." He got his pilot's license before he got his driver's license. Todd and I used to work on a lot of fundamentals in our backyard. I used to throw balls to him in the dirt and he'd cry. I said, "You told me you want to be a ballplayer and if you do, you've got to learn this stuff." He worked hard at it as a kid.

I know the satisfaction of playing that position. There are so many nuances that go on, and you are in on every pitch. A pitcher can have a twitch in his eye and you know something's not right. Other guys, the pitch is thrown and the ball is fouled off, and they mosey around and daydream. When you're a catcher, you've got to be focused on that field. On every hitter, you can see him make an adjustment—just an inch the way he sets his feet up or where he puts his front foot when he goes after the pitch. It's part of that position that comes with the territory. You don't have that anywhere else.

Physically, I think people understand, but mentally, I don't think people comprehend what it's like being behind that plate and trying to get a pitcher through a ballgame. Some days you just say, "This is going to be a long day," and somehow or another you get through it. All the pitchers get all the glory for it.

Ferguson Jenkins

Ferguson Jenkins was that rare pitcher who was able to disregard Wrigley Field's reputation as a hitter's ballpark and make it his own turf. He won 20 games in six consecutive seasons, beginning in 1967, and completed 140 of his 236 starts in that stretch. Although Jenkins didn't start pitching until he was 16 years old, his motion was so easy and uncomplicated that it looked as if he had been throwing from the mound since birth. Leo Durocher made him a starter shortly after Jenkins was acquired from Philadelphia on April 21, 1966, in exchange for Bob Buhl and Larry Jackson. "I had a rubber arm," Jenkins says. "And I liked to pitch." It showed. He was elected to the Hall of Fame in 1991 and was the Cubs pitching coach in 1995 and 1996.

I'd been taught in the minor leagues and that's very important, because in the minor leagues you learn how to pitch in small ballparks. Bad lighting, bad facilities. Now I get to the big leagues and the facilities are great, but they're very small. Connie Mack was a very small stadium. Cal McLish and Al Widmar were my Phillies major league pitching coaches. They used to always tell me you can't give up a number of hits in the inning or you're in trouble. Pitching out of the stretch is tough to do. My first coach ever was Andy Seminick, who said, "Never give in to the hitter. You've got to throw him strikes. You've got to make the hitter do half the work."

Cal McLish taught me the sinker and Al Widmar taught me the slider, and those two pitches got me to the big leagues in the '60s.

To stay there, I had to be consistent and had to work on control and changing speeds. But by far, control—keeping the ball down, down and away, and not letting the hitter have both sides of the plate—gave me the opportunity to learn to pitch in the Phillies organization. All I did was transfer it from there to the Cubs organization and Wrigley Field, and I made Wrigley Field pitcher-friendly for Ferguson Jenkins.

These youngsters today, they don't learn how to pitch. You learn how to pitch in the minor leagues. You can't do anything about the weather, you can't do anything about the wind. The No. 1 thing you can do is you have to know what to do when you're out there, and the composure of learning how to pitch should have been taught to you in the minor leagues. And then you transfer it to what you're going to do and you execute it in a small ballpark like Wrigley Field.

I never let the wind bother me. I didn't look at the flags. I knew I had to face guys like [Willie] Mays, and [Pete] Rose, and [Tony] Perez, and [Johnny] Bench, and [Willie] McCovey, and [Roberto] Clemente. I had no power to stop them from hitting, but I used to make them hit certain pitches they didn't want to hit. I made them swing at pitches they didn't want to swing at. I made ball-clubs first-ball-hitting teams. In my estimation, you have to make the hitters swing at pitches. If you throw seven or eight pitches to each hitter, pretty soon the pitch count is going to be astronomical. I used to make guys swing at first or second pitches. I used to have five-, six-pitch innings. You don't have to strike people out to make them swing at the ball. Today, when you throw 85, 90 pitches for a complete ballgame, it's kind of unheard of. I did that when I played. An hour-and-20-minute ballgame, an hour-and-30-minute ballgame against guys like [Steve] Carlton, and [Tom] Seaver, and [Don] Sutton, and [Bob] Gibson, and [Juan] Marichal.

These young men who pitch now I don't think are pitchers. They're still throwers. Thirty-five- or 40-pitch innings. And before the fifth inning comes along, you're into the 85-, 90-pitch situation. Then the manager wants to take you out of the ballgame.

I remember the black cat game at Shea Stadium in '69 when the black cat walked in front of the dugout. I had a lead in that ballgame and ended up losing it. Later on, I had a game at Shea Stadium, and Don Young made a couple of miscues unfortunately and we end up losing that ballgame. I had a one- or two-run lead in that game, and we ended up losing in a walk off.

Kenny Holtzman pitched some great ballgames and I charted a couple of them, a couple of no-hitters that he pitched against Atlanta and also Cincinnati. You look at these games, and you highlight them in your brain, and you can recall them. But you know, we had a six-and-a-half-, seven-game lead and it diminished. We didn't have a bullpen. Our bullpen was older. If we had had a younger bullpen, I think by far we would've won that particular year. We had a much better ballclub in 1970 with Hickman in the outfield and Pepitone at first base.

We had Kenny Holtzman, Bill Hands, myself, Dick Selma, Rich Nye. We had left- and right-handed pitching. Hitting—if you asked Ernie Banks, Billy Williams, or Ron Santo—hitting is done on a level of seeing the pitches. You can't win with five right-handed starters. You cannot win like that at Wrigley Field. You have to have left-handed pitching. I tried to get left-handed pitching and it just didn't happen. We had Randy Myers for a while out of the bullpen, and we had Bob Patterson, but we didn't have a solid starter, someone who could win 10, 13 ballgames.

It wasn't frustrating as a pitching coach. The only guy who really listened I think was Jaime Navarro. Jaime had some great years when he was here and unfortunately, when he left and went to the White Sox, things kind of changed for him. I used to promote getting ahead of the hitter. Think about what you're doing. Think about it on the bench. You know, the manager of the ball-club sends the first four or five hitters to the plate and those are probably the best hitters in the lineup. Those are the guys who give you the most problems. You've got to get these fellas out to send a message to the bottom half of the lineup that you're on your game that particular day so it'll work. You've got to continue to do it. You don't want to face the good hitters four times. You want to face them a total amount of maybe three. If they go 1 for 3, fine. If they go 2 for 3, fine—if they don't hurt you. But if a guy comes up four times, he's going to get to you. If he comes up five times, you're probably in the shower.

It's not simple. It's execution. You have to learn to pitch in the minor leagues and then bring all that method to the big leagues. But a lot of these guys don't have the opportunity. They get them to the big leagues too quick. They really haven't learned what they should be learning, which is the art of pitching. And the art of pitching is not easy to do. It's tough.

In '69, we were close-knit. Everybody knew one another, I think, because we started to play together in the early '60s. We had Billy, Ronnie, Ernie, Beckert, and Kessinger, and then Hickman came on the scene. We got a chance to know one another. It was a very small clubhouse. An integral part of that was having closeness. I don't think anybody was bitter about this guy's ability or that guy's ability. And by far, we didn't make any money, so nobody was jealous of our salaries. We didn't make squat back in those days. It was terrible. I would rather have a million-dollar contract than $65,000. We didn't make any money. I think everybody understood we were trying to win a championship for the Cubs and for the city. We got close but it just didn't happen.

Leo kind of conveyed from the spring what you've got to have in any kind of sport because you play so many games. You're going to lose a third of them. You know that. So you've got to try to win 90-plus to win your division. That was our goal—which we did, but we ended up second. People don't remember second place, but in our case they do. Why? I've got no idea. It's just the mystique of being the Chicago Cubs. I've got no idea why. We should've played Baltimore in that Series. We were a second-place team people remember.

I enjoyed pitching at Wrigley Field. It was fun. I played in a small ballpark, and I learned how to pitch in a small ballpark. It's a psychological thing, too. If you have a fear of mountains, you can't be a mountain climber. If you have a fear of pitching in small ballparks, you're not going to do well. I didn't fear Wrigley Field. I enjoyed pitching there.

I knew what my job was. I had capable fellows defensively behind me in Kessinger, Beckert, Ernie, and Santo at third. When Ryne Sandberg came up as a rookie and [Larry] Bowa, I knew what their capabilities were. I knew they could do the job. I had to do my job. And my job was to pitch—make the hitter swing the bat and hope the outcome would be good that particular day.

I played against the best ballplayers who ever played the game. I had the chance to face Hank Aaron, Willie Mays, Johnny Bench, Pete Rose, Joe Morgan, Dick Allen. Then when I went to the American League, I had the chance to face Al Kaline, and Harmon Killebrew, and Rod Carew. I faced the best players to ever play the game in my career. People say, "Oh Fergie, if you were born 10, 15 years later." But I might not have played as well. I might not have been as motivated.

Ken Holtzman

On August 19, 1969, Wrigley Field was packed with 41,000 fans. The Cubs were playing Atlanta, the wind was blowing in. Ken Holtzman was the Cubs' starting pitcher and had a no-hitter going. In the seventh, Hank Aaron hit a long fly ball that without that wind would've cleared the fence. Holtzman did not strike out a batter in the game and worked with two different catchers, Bill Heath and Gene Oliver. After that game, the Cubs went 15–25 to go from seven and a half games up in the standings to eight games back. Holtzman, who might have been baseball's second-best Jewish left-hander, remembers the no-hitter.

I've heard that before, that that game was the pinnacle. You obviously can't pinpoint any particular game as the cause. That just coincided with the Mets playing .750 baseball.

It was standing room only and we had just come off a trip. We had something like a seven- or eight-game lead, and we had been in first place most of the year. Cub fever was all over the city. You couldn't get through the crowd to park your car. We parked next to the fire station, and you could hardly get in through the crowd. It was absolutely packed. The people were yelling during batting practice, and Dick Selma was leading the bleacher bums. The whole atmosphere was kind of nuts. The excitement carried over to the players.

It was one of those days where fate smiles on you. Hank Aaron hits a ball that the wind blows back, and that saves the game. The fans are so close, and you can hear what's being said in the first 20 rows. I knew I had it going from the first inning on. It wasn't the players, it was the fans calling your attention to it. You could hear the buzz, you could hear the talk, "You know you got a no-hitter going." It was a close game. The score was 3–0, and we got all our runs in one inning. Plus everything's important on August 19.

I didn't strike out anyone, and I don't think I walked too many guys either. It was almost a perfect game without striking anybody out and without walking anybody. They were hitting the ball a lot on the first or second pitch. They would swing at the first pitch. I didn't throw many pitches that day.

When you pitch a long time at Wrigley Field, you can tell when a ball's going to go out of the park. Aaron's ball blew a little toward the foul line, and it finally came down where that little recess is where the wall curves and Billy stuck his glove up and caught it. The crowd is going crazy. If that happens, you think something's going on. The gods must be looking in on the game. I've always said a no-hitter is just a well-pitched game with a lot of luck.

Aaron grounded out to Beckert to end the game. He was so nervous, he almost couldn't throw the ball to first base. He told me that for the next 30 years.

Randy Hundley was the regular catcher. He caught an average of 150, 155 games—I think he set a record for games caught—and he didn't catch either one of my no-hit games. That's what was even stranger. Bill Heath broke his hand in the sixth or seventh inning, and Gene Oliver finished the game. I'd pitched to both in the bullpen, so it was no big deal. Heath broke his hand and Gene walks out to the mound and he obviously knows what's going on and I think he said, "Whatever you're doing, you're doing it right."

I said, "Just put your fingers down and let's go."

I think you have to have real good stuff to pitch at Wrigley consistently. You can't be a finesse-type pitcher. Eventually you're going to make a pitch, and somebody will hit a cheap home run. Now they play a few night games, but when I pitched there, if I didn't really take care of myself I would lose too much weight over the year. When I was traded to Oakland, I never felt that way in August or September. I always had my best records in August and September and the postseason. I felt when I was with the Cubs, it would take so much out of me physically. I had to watch myself a lot of times to make sure I didn't lose too much weight.

I asked to be traded at the end of the '71 season. My opinion, knowing what I did from players and other teams and organizations, was that the Cubs weren't doing things the way I felt were needed to win. I didn't mean to say the Cubs weren't great to their players. We were among the most well paid, and Mr. Wrigley was first-class to the players and always was. I got in the game to win rings, not travel on charters. I felt I wasn't going to win a ring, regardless of the three or four Hall of Fame players on the team, unless they changed their philosophy. I found out after I left that I was right. I played on two of the greatest teams in history in Oakland and saw what you had to do to win. It took 25 guys.

Leo and I had problems from the standpoint that I felt he took me out of games too soon. I got along with Leo. I still started all the time. It was just one of those things.

I owe Leo a lot for getting me into the major leagues quick. He gave me a chance right away at age 20. I told him that. I was always indebted. After I was in the league four, five years, I told him it was time to let me go. It wasn't because of Leo that I asked to be traded.

The newswriters used to write that I wanted to be the next Koufax because of the obvious similarities. Absolutely not. I do think I'm the last National League pitcher to beat him in '66. You're talking about a guy who retired when he was 27–9. Today that gets you $30 million a year. He was the greatest.

One of my first road trips was in '65. The Cubs were to face Koufax that day, and I threw BP [batting practice] because they wanted a left-hander to assimilate what they would see in a game. I threw pretty hard. That was the game he threw a perfect game against us. That was the game our pitcher threw a one-hitter and lost.

I'm watching this, 27 up and 27 down. Guys are coming back to the dugout, talking to themselves, "I didn't see that pitch." He was the best I ever saw.

I do know I was a better hitter than he was. I have more World Series hits than he does.

Phil Regan

Phil Regan was one strike away from a win against Pittsburgh on September 7, 1969, at Wrigley Field. But Willie Stargell homered into the wind and onto Sheffield Avenue to tie the game, and the Pirates won in extra innings. It was a pivotal game in '69. A key part of manager Leo Durocher's bullpen that year, Regan survived Stargell's blast, even though the Cubs didn't. Regan became the Cubs' pitching coach in 1997, and the next season his prize pupil was a young right-hander named Kerry Wood, who won 1998 Rookie of the Year honors. Regan recalls the big '69 game, as well as why Wood almost didn't finish his 20-strikeout game in May 1998.

It was a big game for us, really. I remember that day because the wind was blowing in a ton. You wouldn't think you could hit a ball out. I'd thrown Stargell a couple of strikes. He fouled a couple off. I threw him a pitch that to me was not a bad pitch, but it was low and in. He hit a line drive up into right field and you know, whenever he hit it, it was gone. He hit it right down the line and it jumped out of there. It was a big game for us. Probably I made the mistake in pitching to him. He hit a fairly good pitch for me. It was down and in, and it was not a bad pitch, but we should've pitched him away with the way the wind was blowing like it was. It was a big game because we were at home, and we always won at home and then we were going into Shea.

What it all came down to was that the team was kind of in disarray. Everybody talked about how we had too many endorsements. We didn't have a lot of endorsements. There were placemats with the International House of Pancakes. Players just signed their names and never made any appearances. The Jewel store did something with our names on glasses. I was the player rep at that time and it all came into one bank. Each player got $2,000 or $5,000 at the end of the year. You couldn't get a lot of endorsements because you played day games. You didn't have time for it.

The biggest thing for me was that we had eight or nine guys who played regular all year long, and I think the biggest thing was that they were tired. And we didn't hold up under the pressure. The Mets kept winning. They couldn't do anything wrong. I've talked to a lot of their players. When we were nine and a half games up in August, they said they thought there was no way they'd catch us. And they started winning and winning, and we started losing and losing. That's the way it is when you go through a slump like that. There's not one person who I think you can point a finger at. It was the entire team. We just didn't play well.

Leo was not a guy who played young kids. He liked veteran players. He was not good with guys like Jim Colborn, or Joe Decker, or guys like that. They all had great stuff, but he didn't care for them because they were young. At the end, he had a lot of confidence in Jim Hickman, who was a veteran, and Paul Popovich. You had Santo, and Beckert, and Kessinger, and Banks; Hundley caught most of the games. They played almost every day.

In '70, I didn't have as good a year as I did in '69. In the first half of '70, I was in a lot of games, and I think I was 10–5 at the All-Star break with a lot of saves. It probably was at a point at that particular time in '69 or '70 when I maybe started losing it a little bit. You don't think you do. My stuff was still the same. I made good pitches, but guys, instead of grounding out or striking out, they'd hit a line drive. I'd think, boy, that's a good pitch. In the middle of the year, I started losing the snap in my slider.

I never felt it was that tough to pitch at Wrigley—maybe because I was a sinkerball pitcher. I never thought about home runs—until Stargell hit that one. I didn't give up a lot of home runs, so it didn't bother me.

You have to be a certain type of pitcher. To win there, you have to be an overpowering pitcher like Fergie, or have great control like Bill Hands, or be a sinkerball pitcher. Kerry Wood can win there because he's overpowering. You get some guys who are

86, 85 miles an hour and it's tough. When the wind's blowing out, you get the ball up and the fences are not that far away.

I think Kerry Wood can come back. Steve Karsay had the same operation and after a year and half, he came back and was throwing 98 miles an hour and said he felt better than he did before the operation. I think Kerry's going to feel better. There were times when he wouldn't throw between starts because his elbow was bothering him. And sometimes we just wouldn't throw. Many times, we'd throw for six minutes. Usually you throw 12 to 15 minutes. And we wouldn't throw any breaking balls. It was almost from the start of the season. It was not something that happened overnight. It was there all the time. A lot of times we wouldn't even throw between starts. He'd go out there and say, "I just can't."

He told me it happened in high school, and every year in the minor leagues they had to shut him down with the same problem. What probably happened was he did pitch more innings, and there was more intensity on the major league level. But I don't think it's something that happened overnight. He's a great competitor, and I think he can come back from that.

It was a big dilemma the day he struck out 20 guys. I told Rigs [Jim Riggleman] we were getting close to 130 pitches. If he had had a long inning, he could've thrown 130 pitches. As it was, he finished with 128. Can you imagine what the people would've said if they'd taken him out if he had one hitter to go and had 19 strikeouts? But we were going to take him out if he had 130 pitches.

It was nice, and I really enjoyed working with the guy. It's amazing, I was with Seattle when Clemens struck out 20, and with Kerry. It's only happened three times, and I was there for two of them.

Arne Harris

*When Arne Harris started directing Cubs broadcasts for WGN in 1964,
he had three cameras to work with. By 2001, he had 12 cameras to pro-
vide television viewers a unique perspective on the game. A die-hard Cub
fan himself, Harris was the voice in the earpieces of Jack Brickhouse,
Vince Lloyd, Harry Caray, Steve Stone, and Harry's grandson Chip
Caray. The "hat shot" was a Harris trademark, part of his endearing
effort to make viewers feel as if they had the best seat in the ballpark. He
died on October 6, 2001, after directing a 13–2 Cubs win.*

The thing that always gets me about Jack Brickhouse is how
upbeat he was. Here's a guy who did the telecast—I didn't join
him until '64, but he did it from '48 until Harry took over in '82—
and he never had a winner. How many guys can go to work every
day for that amount of time and never have a winner? Jack's
biggest moment was '69, and they ended up eight games out of
first place. You've got to marvel at his endurance and the way he
was able to keep his spirit up and keep the telecast going in a
happy mood. We never won. We had a couple years we were hot
for a month or two, so the poor guy had one month every three
or four years, and that was it.

In those days, the thing about Jack is that he was the No. 1 personality in Chicago. I'm convinced that more people knew him
than Mayor Daley. Television then wasn't what it is today. Jack was
on everything. He did band shows, he did politics, he did sports,
he did every show. Jack, really in a sense, in a town where television was just starting to become important, was the person everybody knew.

Harry was different. First of all, Jack built himself into a personality. Harry came to town as a personality. And Harry knew what
he wanted to do. The one thing about Harry—and he was
great—but he caught a couple of breaks. He had a couple pretty

good ballclubs to talk about. The '84 Cubs were fine; the '89 Cubs were fine; and even '85 and '90, they started out well until they had some injuries. He also had a chance to be seen nationwide. Harry knew he was a national personality and he reacted. The old line is that the fox that bit Harry died a long time ago. He was a brilliant guy and very smart. Don't ever underestimate Harry's intelligence. He knew exactly what he was doing and what he had to do, and he was great at it. Jack was great, but Harry was the master at knowing what he had to do, when he had to do it.

That baloney about Harry mispronouncing names, I can't swear to it, but I'm convinced that when things got boring he threw a couple of "Palermos" in there just to shake things up a little bit. What the hell.

People don't know this, but Harry used to look at a tape of a game once in a while. Not all the time, but sometimes. He just wanted some feedback. During the broadcast, I'd tell him something and he'd repeat it. He didn't mind that. He'd talk to me on the air anyway. If he's talking to me, you might as well hear me. Harry had a problem. Maybe it was his ears. The earpieces just didn't work. That's why you could hear me in the background.

How can you not miss Harry? I miss the kidding around. Our big thing—and we did this in front of people—was I'd say, "I made you more famous" and he'd say to me, "No, I made you more famous."

I'd say, "Harry, before you started at 'GN, nobody knew you. You were some announcer with the White Sox and St. Louis. Now, presidents visit you; you own a restaurant; people stop you going through airports."

And he'd say, "Man, before I used your name, nobody knew who you were."

We had more fun with that.

The day he passed away, I had four television trucks in my front yard and I looked up and said, "OK, Harry, you win." How can you not miss Harry? I miss him.

Favorite players? I think Sammy Sosa's the best. He reacts so well, the blowing the kisses and everything. Every time I turn on a sports show with highlights, there's Sammy. I talk to people at ESPN all the time, and they grab our tape because they know they're going to get some stuff. Sammy is so much fun. A couple times, Sammy got so involved in the game he forgot to blow his mother a kiss, so I had the camera guy get the bat boy to run over to get Sammy so he could do it. Sammy remembers most of the time.

For years, when the Cubs were just not a very good team, the only guy they really had was Ernie. We broadcast doubleheaders, and they'd lose 14–3 and 7–1, but Ernie would hit a home run in both games. It was a long day, especially when they'd lose both games. I'd walk out of the truck and I'd figure, ah, the people are mad. And they weren't. They were walking by and saying, "Hey, Ernie hit a home run." Sure, everybody wants to see the Cubs win. You forget sometimes that baseball games are a big deal for some people. They take a year planning a trip to Wrigley Field. Sure, the die-hards are down, but the average guy, hey, he's happy because he saw Ernie hit a home run.

The same thing with Sammy in '97. I'd walk out of the truck and the fans saw Sammy hit a home run or they saw Ryno [Ryne Sandberg] play—you've got to remember that for these people, this is not life or death. This is having a good time. The Cubs have had so many losing years that it creates a situation where very little is needed to make the fans happy. It's a personality thing, too. If you're talking to a Cub fan, I'd say 99 percent revolve around one or two players.

People-wise, there's no other ballpark in the National League where you can get the atmosphere inside and outside the ballpark like Wrigley Field. I can shoot the elevated trains. When things are bad, I can spend three or four minutes shooting people walking in and out of elevated trains. Rooftops, people waving from buildings, lakefront shots, boats and stuff. To me, Wrigley is the best to get the fans, and the ballpark, and everything in the surrounding area.

I'm the luckiest guy in the world. I'm a Cub fan, believe it or not. I'm a North Sider from Chicago. I've had chances to leave and do something else. I don't want to go. If you had told me when I first started in this business that I'd be doing the Cubs for 37 years, I would've told you you were nuts. I'm a Cub fan, and I love them. My wife's a Cub fan, my kids are Cub fans. I love it.

Steve Stone

For 15 seasons, Steve Stone teamed with Harry Caray in the Cubs television broadcast booth. He spent three years analyzing the team with Harry's grandson Chip, then retired after the 2000 season. However, Stone's first introduction to Wrigley Field was as a pitcher in 1974. He was traded to the Cubs from the White Sox with pitchers Ken Frailing and Jim Kremmel and catcher Steve Swisher for infielder Ron Santo. In Stone's three seasons on the North Side, he went 8–6, 12–8, and 3–6. A shoulder injury hindered him in '76, but White Sox general manager Roland Hemond gambled that Stone was OK and re-signed him in 1977. Stone proved he was sound in 1980 with Baltimore when he went 25–7 to win the American League Cy Young Award.

A lot of people don't realize when they talk about the Cubs' 20-game winners that I won 20 games for the Cubs. But it took me three years. I was 23–20 in three years, and the fact is '74, '75, and '76, we didn't make anybody forget about the '27 Yankees. The fact that I was over .500 was a major accomplishment.

One time—it must have been '74—I was in the bullpen. It was one of those days in April when it was absolutely freezing. And Billy Williams was playing first, I do remember that. I was in the pen the whole game. This was before the days when you'd go into the clubhouse to get warm. I was literally frozen solid. So, I got the call to get up. I think it was against the Tigers because I remember the hitter was Tony Taylor. I was taking my warm-up pitches and then Billy Williams came over when Whitey Lockman handed me the baseball and put me in the game. And Billy said, "Are your lips always blue?" I'll never forget that. I said, "I'm just freezing," and I couldn't get loose. I threw one curveball and [Taylor] hit through the left side and the go-ahead run scored, which turned out to be the winning run. That was the end of what was never going to be a wonderful career as a closer. I realized I was going to have to start if I was going to have any success whatsoever.

I had some very good times in 1975. The Cubbies were actually in the race. I started out 5–0. The Cubs were in the race from the middle of June. We had a real interesting collection of guys. George Mitterwald hit three home runs, and it was the highlight of his life because I think he wound up hitting ten for the year, maybe even less than that. We had Carmen Fanzone who was a terrific guy and, unfortunately for Carmen, a better trumpet player than a baseball player. We had Oscar Zamora as our closer, who told our pitching coach Marv Grissom that if he came to the park with his eyes swollen—because he never really had come in at night—that it was the ozone. It wasn't that he was partying all night, it was the ozone. He'd come in with his eyes looking like the old fighter Carmen Basilio. Marv assumed it wasn't the ozone. I think Oscar led our staff with 13, 14 saves. We weren't particularly good, like so many teams I was on, but we had a good time. It was a good bunch of guys. Pete LaCock was around, and Dave Rosello.

Marshall was our third base coach, and he was very sensitive about his hair. As a third base coach, you can mess around with him. We got a mop and cut off the handle and put it in a box. We put his name on it and we were going to present the mop to him. "If you needed a rug or toupe, here, use this because it looks better than what you've got on your head." The day we brought it in to give it to him, he was named manager of the team. Of course, you're not going to do that to the manager of the team. You could do it to the coach, but not the manager. So he was never presented with that mop. His promotion turned out OK.

We always knew when he was coming out to get you on the mound because he'd always pull down the back of his cap, pull down the front of his cap, pull down the back, pull down the front, do it about three times each. Tug on the back, tug on the front to make sure the toupe was right in line. And then he'd go to the mound to get you. There was no mystery. You didn't even have to look in the bullpen. You could tell when you were coming out by how many times he adjusted his cap.

Then, in 1976, I hurt my rotator cuff and nobody could figure out what was wrong. Jim Marshall was the manager. There was a work stoppage almost the first half of spring training—it was either a lockout or a strike—and we had an accelerated spring training. And I tried to accelerate my pitching style to get ready for the season because I was coming off a 12–8 year in '75. I hurt myself. Nobody could really diagnose what it was. I remember Jim Marshall's quote in the paper [there was an article, "Mysterious Arm Ailment Plaguing Stone"]. He said, "He'll feel a lot better when we get to the big ballparks on the West Coast," because that was our first trip.

I just knew my arm was killing me and nobody could tell me what was wrong with it. Marshall starts me against the Dodgers in Los Angeles—the Buckner-Cey-Garvey-Lopes Dodgers—and I faced five hitters. I was throwing almost eephus pitches. The balls were so slow that these guys couldn't believe it. Garvey never hit me. He popped up behind the screen. I think Buckner hit one to the wall. I retired all five hitters. So finally, after five outs, Jim Marshall comes walking out to the mound and he says, "Tell me the truth, how do you feel?"

I said, "Fine, Jim. I'm saving it for the late innings. How do you think I feel?"

He said, "OK," and he took me out of the game and sent me back to Chicago. I went to the doctors and nobody could diagnose it.

Eventually it was diagnosed for me by a guy by the name of Tom Satler, who told me I had a rotator cuff injury. It was the first I had ever heard about that, the first I had ever read about it. He was a professor at the University of Illinois–Circle Campus. He told a friend of mine, "I think I can help Steve." Three months of weight work, no surgery, no drugs, ice. Cryotherapy is what they called it. I would ice and then work out with weights. And then he said it would double the blood flow coming back. Three months. I never had another shoulder problem the rest of my life.

I was the Cubs' first free agent. I was the first guy ever to go without a contract. So the Cubs didn't want to pitch me the second part of the year when I was healthy. They did pitch me in one game. Fortunately, Roland Hemond was in the seats. I threw five innings, gave up two hits and one run, and threw the ball great, and Roland Hemond and Bill Veeck drafted me in that first free-agent draft.

Roland said, "Everybody says you've got a bad arm, but from what I saw it's pretty good."

I said, "I'm fine. I had arm problems, but now it's 100 percent." And I won 15 games for them in 1977.

I spent 15 years with Harry and we never rehearsed an opening. Not one. Ever. Harry wanted one microphone, took the mike, and Arne would go in our ears, "OK." No countdown, just go get 'em. And then Harry would start, "Hello again everybody, Harry Caray," and then he would give me the mike. He wanted one mike so he could control it. There was not even a thought of prep time. I had no idea what he was going to say. I'm not sure if he knew what he was going to say, but I do know sometimes he would say exactly what I was going to say.

You couldn't program Harry. If you told Harry not to say anything, he would say it immediately. He was a contrarian. He was going to do whatever it was he wanted to do, and you couldn't tell him anything.

I thought it was up to me to analyze pitchers. A couple times Harry would go and analyze the pitchers first thing out of the box and then hand the mike to me. I had no idea where he was going and maybe the spontaneity of the thing is what made us.

Jim Marshall

Jim Marshall played for the Cubs in 1958–1959 and eventually retired as a player in '65. In July '74, Marshall was promoted from third base coach to manager, replacing Whitey Lockman. In two full seasons, Marshall's Cubs posted identical 75–87 records. He didn't get much help. Salty Saltwell, an expert on stadium operations, was named general manager in '76, but he returned to his ballpark-only duties after that year and was replaced by Bob Kennedy. Kennedy then fired Marshall. However, Marshall has the distinction of being the last Cubs manager since Leo Durocher to get another major league managing job after being fired by the Cubs. He was named Oakland's skipper in 1979. Why is that?

I don't know the answer except I had to go back to the minors to succeed again to get another pop. With time running out, I had to go back to manage in Japan, and that's what I chose to do. I'd been minor league manager of the year three times. That doesn't do it after a while.

The biggest problem was eliminating the fans' feelings and thoughts about the '69 Cubs and bringing in the Bill Madlocks, and the Pete LaCocks, and several of the players that were no-names. That was probably the most difficult thing of all. And secondly, the most difficult thing was that there was a change in the general manager. And they brought in a fellow who was basically in charge of concessions. We made one trade all year and that sometimes doesn't do it for the guys on the field. That was, I feel, a turning point for me being gone. We moved up a notch every year, good win-loss records against the Cardinals every year, and those are the things that I think about.

From a pitcher's standpoint, I think the most difficult thing in that era was to be a pitcher. We had some good young pitchers. [Bill] Bonham and [Rick] Reuschel would come into my office after losing 1–0 and 2–1, and they were so frustrated. They didn't know what to do. We didn't have a legitimate No. 4 hitter or a legitimate 3 or 4. We tried to move Rick Monday into that spot, but when you have to say Jerry Morales or Jose Cardenal is your fourth hitter, you've got problems. That's not a knock against their abilities. It just wasn't fair to put them in that position.

The thing I felt about the Cubs was that you had to have depth in your pitching staff more than any other ballpark. If you don't have extra pitchers, you're going to get killed in that ballpark. I shared that with Don Baylor in [his first] spring training. So, welcome home. That's why I'm in Albuquerque.

If I had to pick one single thing, by far that's it. The ballpark. I don't think people realize it. People are building them now where it's easier to hit home runs again. You need more pitchers because of the size of the park, there's no doubt about it. Many times I brought a pitcher in, and I knew the guy I brought in was not as good as the one I was taking out.

Ernie always remembers my wife and all my childrens' names, and I don't see him that much. When I first joined the Cubs, we were playing the Giants in Wrigley Field. Ernie and I were both in the lineup and we had scored a lot of runs. The next day the pitcher was Gomez, and he decided to throw at everybody, and he got Ernie and hit him in the hip and leg area. The clubhouse was up a flight of stairs, and Ernie had to use a cane; he could barely make it. I thought to myself, "He'll never make it."

Sure enough, the next day, no infield, no batting, no nothing, and he hobbles out in the first inning and he hits a grand-slam his first time at bat. There's no modern-day player who would've played. I'll never forget that day. He was a gamer.

Jose Cardenal

In spring training 1975, Jose Cardenal complained that he was unable to sleep because a noisy cricket in his room had kept him awake. Chicago Tribune *columnist Mike Royko wrote about that and about how Cardenal was fearful that he would miss starting on Opening Day because one of his eyelids was stuck shut. Royko called Cardenal "an inspiration to those of us who believe in sleeping late, walking slow, and calling in sick at the office." Cardenal just shakes his head in disbelief when asked about the eyelid incident. The personable outfielder made six consecutive Opening Day starts, beginnng in 1972. Cardenal talks about what happened with his eyes, baseball's good old days, and why he left Chicago.*

It was about three days before Opening Day and in Arizona, there's a lot of dust and it had created a little infection in my left eye. It was bothering me, so I took the dust out and I couldn't open my left eye. I didn't play the last three games in spring training, and they sent me home and they cleaned my eyes and I was fine. People make it like I came from space; I don't want to do this, I don't want to play. Royko talked about it, Royko wrote about it.

I used to do things to entertain the kids and the ladies. It's like what Sammy Sosa is doing now. You want to make the fans happy, you do different things, clown around. That's when baseball used to be baseball, back when baseball was fun. Now things are different. Nobody has fun anymore.

I used to juggle balls in the outfield between innings. You see a lot of people warming up on the side. I used to get three balls and play around with it. I was warming up.

I played the violin one time for Jack Brickhouse. I'd never played the violin before. Somebody took one to my house and I started playing with it, and a few notes just came, I don't know how. And I played for half an hour. It was fun. That's when baseball was fun.

Herman Franks and Bob Kennedy—one was the field manager and one was the general manager—and they ran me out of town for no reason. Why? I have to say jealousy. I was very popular—I still am in Chicago. It was 1971; Bob Kennedy was the minor league farm director with the Cardinals. This was the same year I was wearing my afro in St. Louis. I guess Mr. Kennedy didn't like that. He didn't have nothing to do with me because he was the minor league farm director, so I told him just leave me alone, go ahead take care of your minor league kids and leave me alone. He said, "OK, I'll remember that."

Six years after, he was the GM in Chicago, and I know when I heard that they named him the GM, I knew I didn't have a chance. I was 100 percent right. He didn't want to play me, and he told Herman Franks not to play me. He remembered what had happened six years back. Six years later, he was in power. In this game, you never know.

I wasn't playing at all, he wanted to trade me to Philadelphia and I refused because I was 10 and 5. I didn't want to go nowhere. So finally, they don't play me at all. During the winter in 1977, I realized I was going to have to go to another team, so I went to Philadelphia.

My dream was to finish my career in Chicago and it never happened. Today, I never forget it. I feel hurt. I was very well known in Chicago, and I was a popular person in Chicago. I still live in the city. Chicago's my home.

Chicago is like New York. Either they like you or they don't like you. When I was in the National League in St. Louis, I used to kill the Cubs all the time and the fans couldn't stand me. Two years later, I was with the team and they opened their hearts to me.

Bill Madlock

The Cubs dealt popular pitcher Ferguson Jenkins to Texas to acquire a rookie third baseman named Bill Madlock, who the team hoped would replace Ron Santo. That's tough duty to replace two local legends. Madlock fared well, winning consecutive batting titles in 1975 and 1976. He didn't clinch the second title until the last day of the season, beating Ken Griffey, Sr., with a 4-for-4 day. Despite his success and youth, Madlock was dealt to San Francisco in February 1977. He believes money wasn't the only reason the Cubs were motivated to trade him.

It was the last game of the season in '76 and I had been out because I got mugged in New York the week before. I was out three or four days, but I came back to play the last three games. Going into the last game of the season it was something like a three-point difference between Griffey and myself. What I wanted to do—I figured I had no chance of winning—but I wanted to hit over .340. They were at home, and we were at Chicago, and a friend of mine called and said, "You've got a chance."

And I said, "No, I don't have a chance."

And she said, "OK, go 4 for 4."

The first time up, I think I got a base hit. The next time up, the infield was in and I hit a little blooper over the first baseman's head. And at that time, Griffey and I were tied, so they were going back and forth calling Cincinnati, and they were announcing it in Chicago. The next time up, I bunted for a base hit and then I took the lead, and all this time Griffey wasn't playing. So, they found out I had taken the lead and they put Griffey in the game and I guess he struck out. My next time up I got a double off the wall. So, I was three or four points ahead of him.

I think Cincinnati batted around so it was over if he didn't get that at bat. I think they sent nine men to the plate, because he made the last out and he struck out. I was at home when I heard that I won it.

I was only thinking of staying over .340. That's a lot of points to make up the last game of the season. I found out Pete Rose and Joe Morgan told Griffey to sit down. He should've sat down the day before. I think whoever was the Cy Young pitcher that year pitched the next-to-last day of the season, and Griffey played that day and went 0 for 4.

I always think hit. That's the whole thing. I'm always thinking, "I'm better than that pitcher out there, regardless of who it is." If someone gets me out 100 times, they've got to work twice as hard to get me out that 101st time. I always believed in myself as a hitter. I was never satisfied. I talked to Pete Rose and some other hitters, and they were never satisfied. I see some of these guys now, if they get one hit, they're satisfied. If they go 1 for 10 every game and they got their one—hell, if I got one, I wanted two. If I got two, I wanted three. All of the good hitters are like that. They're never satisfied. And you've got to work to get them out.

It had to be '74 or '75. Al Hrabosky used to do that patting the glove and walking around the mound, you know. He'd do that shit and when he gets up there on the mound, I walked out. And then when I got up in the box, he went back. This went on—well, it was probably only a couple of minutes, but it seemed like forever—and all of a sudden, the umpire said, "Throw," and I was out of the box getting pine tar, which I never used anyway, and he started throwing, and the umpire started calling strikes. Jim Marshall jumped in the batters box. Jose Cardenal jumped in the batters box. I jumped in the batters box. And all of a sudden, Hrabosky let one go and it almost hit Jim Marshall in the head. And then I got back in the box, and [Ted] Simmons and I start yelling at each other and all of a sudden I smoked him, and then all hell broke loose. This was a fight, this wasn't a grabbing or anything. This was a fight. I think that's the only thing we had going for us. We had good fighters on the team. It seems like we fought for half an hour. It was just a rivalry between the Cubs and Cardinals.

I think what happened with the Cubs is that I probably came up at the wrong time. Wrigley was very, very old-fashioned. Ernie, Billy—when you think of the Cubs, you think of those two guys. They're two of the greatest to ever play the game. But when I came up it was different. Ernie, he did what he had to do. I'm not a rah rah, let's play two. That's Ernie, fine and good. I love him, but that's just not me. Billy, he's the quiet type, except when he gets that bat in his hand. And I'm me. And I'm different than all of them. I'm a little more outspoken. The times of baseball were changing, and they were going through the multiyear contract. [Wrigley] said, "I didn't pay Billy, I didn't pay Ernie, so I'm not going to pay you." So, what does that tell you?

They didn't mention any of the white players that they didn't pay, it was always Billy and Ernie. So, was it race? It wasn't stats. So, you've got to look at it some way. I don't know. You can make the decision yourself because obviously, coming after winning two batting titles with a team that wasn't going anywhere and you trade for a guy—Bobby Murcer is a good ballplayer. But I was five or six years younger, and I was just starting out and had just won two batting titles. I know we didn't win, but I did a lot for the Cubs for the three years I was there.

I guess that speaks for itself right there. It's a very conservative organization. Wrigley was Wrigley. I think they wanted every black player to be like Ernie and Billy. And that's unfair. It's unfair to say they want every black player to be like me or every white person to be like you. It was a very conservative organization.

I was 20-something years old and I thought I'd be with Chicago forever, you know, and it didn't work out that way. One thing you find out early in baseball is that sometimes it's not the stats that you put up. You see some strange things happen in this game. That's just a part of the game. It happens now, it'll happen forever.

I didn't want a $1 million contract. That was the year that the multiyear started. They didn't do it for Ernie, they didn't do it for Billy, and that's what it came down to.

I've been told this, too—that I came there in a bad situation at the beginning because they got rid of two of their favorites just so I could play. They traded Fergie and they traded Santo so I could play, and I think that might have had something to do with it. In Chicago, it's family oriented, 150 games on TV. When I was in Chicago, the fans act like you're their long-lost buddy and the reason for that is because you see them every day on TV. They were the superstation when there was no superstation.

I was just learning how to hit in Wrigley Field. I think I could've put up tremendous stats in Wrigley Field because to me, you have to learn how to hit there. The wind affects your swing so much there, but it never affected mine. I never would change and try to hit the ball out of the ballpark because the wind was blowing out or try to change because it was blowing in. That was one thing, I was just learning how to hit there. But after that, I was gone.

Mike Krukow

Whenever Mike Krukow returns to Wrigley Field, he has a flashback to September 1976 when the right-handed pitcher was first called up. Just getting to the ballpark for his big league debut was an experience. Krukow pitched for some poor Cubs teams from 1976 to 1981 and finished above .500 only once (in 1978), when he was 9–3. He later starred with the San Francisco Giants, winning 20 games in 1986. He's sentimental about his days with the Cubs—as he should be.

Probably one of the most unique things about Wrigley Field—and I don't know if too many people ever talk about this—but it's probably one of the only places in the world where if a guy comes up in September, a hitter, and you don't know anything about him, you can sit down in the bullpen and ask the fans. They'll know. That's how good and knowledgeable they are about the game.

When you're in the bullpen, it's like you're in the stands with the fans and you're having a conversation. They'd ask you about guys, and you'd ask them about guys, and what you thought their opinion was. I thought the interaction was really fun.

It was the very first ballpark I walked into as a big leaguer, and I'll never forget it. I didn't even know how to get to the ballpark. I got to the Executive House after four years in the minor leagues. I went down and got a cab and hopped into the backseat, and I told the driver, "Wrigley Field."

And she said, "How do I get there?"

I said, "I have no idea."

After about a half-hour ride, we finally pull up and she dropped me off on the right field side, which is the visitor's side. I went in there and I walked up the ramp. I walked into the gate right there by the right field bullpen, and I walked across the field because it was early, it was about 8:30.

From the time I got onto the field and walked all the way into the left field corner where the entrance to the Cubs clubhouse was, I was crying like a baby. It was the most excited I'd ever been as an athlete. And there wasn't anybody in the stands. That's one of the memories I'll always take with me. What better place to walk into for the first time? It was green as green could be. I floated all day long. I got in the game—Jim Marshall was the skipper—and it was magic. And it stayed that way, even in the years that we didn't do well, and there were a lot of them in the late '70s, early '80s. I still had great pride to wear that uniform and it was a wonderful place to play.

I think everybody should have the pleasure of playing in that ballpark for that city for that organization for one year in their career—that's how good it is.

Bruce Sutter

When Bruce Sutter was the Cubs' closer, he would pitch two or three innings in a game. In 1977, he compiled a 1.35 earned run average with 31 saves, although he missed six weeks because of injury. Sutter and his famous split-finger pitch led the National League in saves in '79 with 37, and he won the Cy Young Award. The right-hander took the Cubs to arbitration after that season and won, but the financially shocked Cubs dealt him to St. Louis in December 1980, and he led the league in saves for three more seasons. On June 23, 1984, Sutter came on in relief to face a young Cubs infielder named Ryne Sandberg—twice.

I signed with the Cubs as a free agent and I could throw pretty hard and had a decent curve. My first two years, they were teaching me how to throw the slider. Fred Martin was the pitching coach. I tried to throw the slider, and I popped something in my elbow. I took the rest of the summer off, and they told me to let it rest over the winter. I started throwing the next year to get ready for spring training, and it still hurt. I had a pinched nerve, and I had an operation. So, I went to spring training. I'd had my arm out of a cast a week and a half, and I didn't say anything, and I started throwing like the rest of the pitchers. I didn't tell anybody about it.

It came time to start playing in games and I didn't want to throw the slider, it made my elbow hurt. I talked to Fred and he said try this [the splitter]. He didn't just show me the split, he showed a lot of pitchers. For me, it was more one finger on top. Donnie Moore was the other pitcher who used it as his main pitch. I just wanted to get the hitters out.

In '76, I was the set-up man. I'd come in in the sixth and seventh and set up Mike Garman and Darold Knowles. They'd just brought me up. By the end of that year, there was one time

Darold and I were both warming up in Cincinnati, and Joe Morgan was coming in to hit. Darold was a left-hander, and Morgan was a left-handed hitter. They brought me in to face the star hitter, and Darold said he knew his job as a closer was over then.

I finally felt like I belonged in '77. We had a lot of fun in the beginning. Everything kind of clicked and we won a bunch of games and we were in first place a lot of times. I pitched so much. I think I had 75 innings by the All-Star break. I pulled a muscle under my armpit before the All-Star Game. I'd gotten picked for the game at Yankee Stadium, but I didn't pitch again until August. I was out six weeks. I ended up with 31 saves. The save record at that time was 38. If I'd pitched those six weeks, I would've shattered that.

A lot of times, you'd come in in the seventh inning for the save. We got used to doing that. It meant that there were some days they didn't have me available. The games dictate themselves. We had a good pitching staff when I was with the Cubs. Everybody maligned us. You look at the names on the '77, '78, '79 Cubs pitching staff, and a lot of us played 10, 12 years.

A lot of people think of me as a Cub. I was traded. And the way the whole thing transpired, I wanted to sign a four-, five-year contract. I had agreed to it with Bob Kennedy. We went down to the Wrigley Building, and Mr. Wrigley thought it was too much money. So, we filed for arbitration. I had nothing to lose. We went in at $700,000, and the Cubs went in at $350,000. I would've signed for four or five years for $350,000 at that time. We won at $700,000. That threw eveything out of whack, their whole pay scale. It was just a matter of time before they traded me.

I was just sitting there at the meeting. I like to go to some of those just because you want to hear what's said. I just sat back. Mr. Wrigley just thought it was too much money to pay a baseball player. He didn't think it was right the Cubs would pay deferred money when I wasn't going to play anymore. It was the kind of deal where Bob Kennedy's face got red. Here he is the general manager, and we'd agreed to a deal.

That was one of the first big cases. It broke everybody's back. I won the Cy Young that year. The owners thought arbitration would be a good deal for them and after that, they decided it wasn't so good.

In '84, I'm with the Cardinals, and the Cubs and Cardinals are big rivals. We come into Chicago and we get there late. I'm in bed and the phone rings 3:00, 4:00 in the morning. I pick up the phone and this guy says, "If you pitch tomorrow, I'm going to kill you." That morning, I talk to the traveling secretary and tell him somebody called me last night and said if I pitch today, they're going to kill me. I thought it was just some drunk. They say, "Well, we better check it out." They talk to the police and the FBI. And there are [security] guys sitting in the stands near the bullpen.

Now, Ryne pulls off a little bit and steps toward third base a little bit. Any hitter who does that gave me problems. Jack Clark, Pedro Guerrero, and Ryne Sandberg. My ball went down and in to right-handers. I know that.

I'm trying to keep the ball away from him or if I come inside, get him to swing over the top of it. I let up a little bit and Ryne hits a homer. I go, "Wow." OK, Willie McGee is having a great day that day. He hits for the cycle. They tie the game up and Ryne comes up again. Well, I'm thinking I've got to pitch him the same way. Ryne was a double threat. If you walked him, he'd steal second. That made him a double tough player. Some of the guys who hit home runs, I could walk those guys because they didn't steal. Where he batted in the lineup, you walked him and he stole second, and you had to pitch to the third- and fourth-place hitters. Hell if I didn't throw it to the same spot, and he hit another one.

We lose the game and the FBI guys are there. They say, "Shit, we better stay with you." I go back to my hotel room and order room service. They call and ask if I've gotten any more phone calls. I say yeah, and [this time] they said if I don't pitch tomorrow, they're going to kill me.

Rick Monday

*In the bottom of the fourth inning of a Cubs game on April 25, 1976, at
Los Angeles, a man and his 11-year-old son jumped from the stands and
ran onto the field. Rick Monday will tell the rest of the story. He takes
great pride in what he considers a natural reflex. Monday was considered
the team's first legitimate center fielder since Andy Pafko 20 years earlier.
Monday, who played for the Cubs from 1972 to 1976, was impressed by
Chicago's fanaticism and batted .294 with 20 home runs in '74, but it's a
flag-saving grab that he's best remembered for.*

The thing that got my attention, quite frankly, is when I flew into
town—it may have been in January—and there was a press conference and I think a stockholders' meeting in Chicago. From the
airport to downtown, you listen to cab drivers give you the
update on what's happening in sports. I didn't identify myself, and
the driver was talking about how the Cubs just made this deal.

So, when I went around the city, everywhere I went, everyone
was talking about sports in this town and they were talking about
the Cubs. I said, wait a minute. This is a ballclub that has not
really had a great deal of success, they're still smarting over 1969.
Yet here it is in January, it's five, six degrees outside, and they're
talking about Cubs baseball and they can't wait for spring training
to start. They could name the starting lineup of any particular
sport. That got my attention.

When I got here, people knew about me. I had one guy who
came up to me and said, "You have horses. Here's a place where
you could board your horses." And I'm thinking, I just got done
playing baseball in Oakland, and people there didn't even know
that unless they'd been to the house and seen that we had horses.

You see the following in spring training and then we finally get
into town. You think this is a little unusual and until you're here
for a while, you experience it, you live it, you taste it, and you
hear it, it's difficult to explain to people why it's so unique.

There are some bleacher fans who I still see when I come out to the Cubs Convention in the winter. There was one little group out in right center field that would be yelling and what have you. We had this thing going. I would motion one way and they would lean to the right; and I would motion another way and they would lean to the left; and another way and they'd stand up; and another way and they'd turn around. That was a group that was out there almost every day.

You got to recognize all of the people. You got to recognize their voices when they would say something. I didn't understand this to begin with, but you're either a right field bleacher bum or a left field bleacher bum, and they go their separate ways. They're all out there together for the Cubs, but they live in different neighborhoods, and those are different neighborhoods in right field and left field. I still see some of those people from time to time, and all of a sudden, boom, you go through a time capsule and you're back in the '70s.

I was with the Cubs on a Sunday afternoon in Los Angeles. Bottom of the fourth inning. I was in center field. I think that day Jose Cardenal was playing in left field. I saw out of the corner of my eye two guys come onto the field. I think they entered somewhere near the left field foul pole. They were in very shallow left center field. I saw that one of them had something under his arm, but I couldn't make out what it was. All I knew was that there were a couple people coming onto the field.

Now, the first thing that comes to your mind is, you see a couple guys, you don't know A, if they're out to make a statement; B, if they're out to win a bet with somebody in the stands; or C, maybe they just don't like you and they're going to punch out your lights. I mean, you don't know.

I think back to other times when people have run out onto the field. I remember in Oakland a number of years ago, a guy came out onto the field and he was absolutely blitzed out of his mind.

He shook Mike Hershberger's hand in left field, came by and shook my hand in center, went over and shook Reggie Jackson's in right, and then he realized he could not go to the stands because here comes the onslaught of all the guards. So, they're minimizing the area that he has to roam. And he goes to right center field and he hits the fence on a run, and he starts to go over and he can't lift himself over the fence. Reggie and I go over and we help him up. He gets one leg over on top of the fence; he gets the other leg over on top of the fence, he disappears from our sight, and all we hear from the other side is a thud followed by a groan.

So, these two people stopped in left center and they spread out what proved to be an American flag, and they spread it out on the ground. I started running in that direction. I still don't know what I was thinking, except what they were about to do was not right. They pulled out a can, I could see it reflecting, so I'm thinking lighter fluid. It was. They were dousing it. The wind blew the first match out. Then the photograph that James Roark took— that was nominated for a Pulitzer Prize—shows me taking the flag away and the guy was there with the match. He thought the flag was still there. So he threw the can of lighter fluid at me as I'm running off. Tom Lasorda, who was then the third base coach for the Dodgers, ran by me, and I gave the flag to Doug Rau, a left-handed pitcher with the Dodgers.

So, the game is over, and I said, "When you get through with the court case with these guys, can I have that flag?" The guys were fined $80 a piece and put on two years' probation. When the Dodgers came back into Chicago not too long later, Al Campanis presented it to me, and that flag is now proudly displayed in my home.

I still get letters and, surprisingly enough, most of the letters come from kids who were not even born at the time. There's a couple letters from guys who were in the military; they were in Vietnam and flashing back on that flag. When they were there and they were experiencing a very difficult time, about the only thing they had to hold on to that signified reality at all was that little piece of cloth that some of them carried folded up in their jackets and their pockets.

A gentleman yesterday came up to me and shook my hand. Tears were coming out of his eyes, and he said, "I want to thank you for my father." His father had been a veteran that had been wounded. Without trying to be melodramatic or anything else, the flag represents rights and freedoms that people have given their lives for us to be able to enjoy.

I'm asked sometimes, "Does it bother you to be known for one incident that happened to take place when you were in uniform but not swinging a bat, or catching a ball, or something like that—stopping two idiots from burning a flag?"

My response then and still is, "So, what's wrong with that?"

Jimmy Piersall

To say Jimmy Piersall is a colorful character is a gross understatement. This is a man who celebrated his 100th home run by running the bases backward. In 1977, he joined Harry Caray in the Chicago White Sox broadcasting booth and they became the city's first shock jocks. Piersall's candid style eventually offended White Sox management, and he was fired in '81. In 1985, Cubs general manager Dallas Green—victim of that 100th homer—hired Piersall to be a minor league coach. After 14 years teaching outfielders and hitting fungoes, Piersall was fired in November 1999—probably for being too outspoken.

I was with the Texas Rangers. Harry Caray came into town, and the White Sox said they were looking for somebody to audition with him. I said sure. I needled Harry pretty good. I was doing my thing, and they were very pleased about it. I got a call asking if I was interested in working with Harry, and I said I was. They brought me into Chicago and I had an interview with Bill Veeck. Bill didn't seem too interested in me. Finally, he said, "We don't have much money to work with. We've got $35,000."

I said, "I'll take it."

He could've said $10,000 and I would've taken it.

The next day, they were going to have a press conference and all of a sudden Mayor Daley died. There was no interview. Harry says, "You're off to a good start, kid."

Going to work with Harry wasn't easy. Harry was a great professional. He could announce the game and do the analyzing at the same time. It took me time to learn and understand what he wanted.

Even though I could talk, it was a whole new ballgame for me. I was doing postgame interviews. I had to go downstairs in the eighth inning and, by the time I got somebody, Harry would keep talking and the guy would leave me. And sometimes I wound up with the tarpaulin being thrown over me or the water being turned on. That was the hardest $35,000 I ever made. Finally, his wife, Dutchie, told him one day that I could help change his image. Harry didn't seem to mind what she said and, from that point on, he was more patient with me. He would teach me when to go in and when not to go in, how to study.

Then things got tough. All of a sudden, the White Sox got new ownership. They didn't like Harry, and they couldn't tell Harry and I what to do. It was always, "You're second-guessing," and "You shouldn't do this," and "You shouldn't do that." Harry said to them, "We're first-guessing."

Harry then decided to go to the Cubs, and I got into trouble with the "horny broads" comment, which turned out to be the best thing that ever happened to me. See, I was invited to do a television show with Mike Royko. I said to my wife, "I shouldn't do this. I have a bad feeling about this." I get there, and Harry is ripping away, and Royko says to me, "How come these women [players' wives] want to get you fired?"

I said, "Well, they don't like what I say." Then they were going to commercial, and I said, "They don't know anything about ball, about the game. They're a bunch of horny broads." I let it go at that.

So, the next day I'm coming to the ballpark, and the owner says to me, "We enjoyed the show, we enjoyed it very much." Two days later, they're taking me off the air because Tony La Russa and the players weren't going to play if they didn't take me off the air. Here's a last-place club telling the owner that.

La Russa came after me one night with Jim Leyland and Charlie Lau down at the studio around 12:00. I was doing the talk show after the game. During the game, I was coming on every inning on Channel 44. Nobody saw it anyways. I couldn't see how people could get so excited. Nobody saw it.

Anyways, they came down to the studio, and I said, "What are you doing here?"

And La Russa said, "You're trying to get Leyland fired."

And I said, "What do you mean?"

La Russa said, "You said on the air that we didn't have an outfield coach."

I said, "The way Chet Lemon is throwing the ball all over the place, no communication between infielders and outfielders and between the outfielders themselves, it's terrible."

Leyland was drunk and he tore his shirt out. I wish I'd been about 10 years younger because I would've hit him right in the nose. I said to La Russa, "You better get out of here." I could've called the cops. The owners called me up and apologized to me for what he did. La Russa never apologized.

My consistently telling it like it is was the problem. They made it negative. I didn't make it negative. They were terrible ballplayers. The first year, 1977, was fine when the Sox won 90 games. That helped me, too, because when you're winning, the fans don't get on the announcers. The players never said anything to me, but they didn't like what I was saying. That's too bad. I think that was the turning point when the owner went ahead and fired me. You notice I don't say the owner's name. My wife told me I can't because I have to watch my blood pressure.

You have to be truthful if you know what you're talking about. But today, you've got to be a shill. You can't say things anywhere about anything anymore. Everybody's sensitive and they don't want to hear the truth. Harry and I never even thought about it. We never sat down and talked about what we were going to do. We clowned around. We said as much good things about guys as criticism.

I don't make the fans boo. Most of the time, they're not booing you, they're booing the situation. I can't lie. No, that's not my bag. I can't lie now. Believe it or not, I'm not looking to rip a guy. I love to praise guys. I may have said I didn't think Mike Caruso was ready to play in the big leagues in '98, but I think he proved me wrong. And I said that. But I said that if you noticed, he doesn't have a defensive first baseman to field those balls.

The fans in Chicago have been great to me. I know I can't please everybody. I certainly like to have the fans disagree with me and not like me because that means they listen. They're listening. They have a sort of respect because they want to hear the truth. I'm the only guy in town who can talk baseball on the air the way it should be talked.

Dallas Green gave me a coaching job with the Cubs. He was the guy I hit my 100th home run off of and ran backward, so I didn't know how he would take a meeting with me. I gave him my baseball talk about what I thought I could do, how I could learn to teach, what my ability is and how I enjoy kids. I said, "I'll work for nothing until I can prove I can do the job."

I started, and after about a month or so, Dallas said, "You've got the job. We'll give you about $1,000 a month."

I said, "One thousand dollars for my brains and my knowledge about baseball?"

He said, "What do you want?"

I said, "$2,500."

And he said OK.

Most teams don't specialize with outfielders. They don't put it as important as the infield, and it isn't. But if you watch the majority of outfielders today, they don't make the plays, they don't do the drills. Because they're bad, the fans accept it. Only I know how bad they are. I watch them. They don't set up and react on every pitch; they don't run hard after every ball; they don't back up an infielder when a ground ball is in the infield; they don't holler loud for balls; they don't have infield/outfield practice drills; they don't have balls hit in the gap where they learn how to pick the ball up and how to take their steps and relay.

I don't say major leaguers don't work at all. They just don't pride themselves like I did. I teach my kids to pride themselves. I've got a whole folder of the right way to teach. I also teach them about equipment. It's so important to have proper equipment. They've got to have two gloves, two pairs of shoes, two shirts. They say, "I can't afford it." I say, "You got a car? Sell it."

I've got 14 kids who got to the major league roster. Guys like Rafael Palmeiro, who was an outfielder for me. Dwight Smith, Doug Dascenzo, even Kevin Roberson, Pedro Valdes, Robin Jennings, Doug Glanville. These guys got there. That's my thrill. Those kids give me a hug when they see me.

The Cubs could fire me tomorrow, and they don't owe me nothing. I'm very grateful. The Cubs gave me the opportunity to be around the game I love. Even now, I always work hard because I'm always afraid I might get fired. Especially an outspoken guy. They can fire you in a minute.

Dallas Green

Dallas Green is a large man. Everything about him is large, from his voice to his ego. Green probably changed the course of the Cubs more than any other general manager. Hired by the Tribune Company after it purchased the ballclub in 1981, Green left his precious Philadelphia after guiding the Phillies to a world championship in 1980. He revamped the team, the front office, the attitude—everyone and everything. The Cubs won the National League East in 1984 because of the rebuilding under Green. Fans can only wonder what might have happened if he had stayed rather than abruptly left in October 1987 because of "philosophical differences." To this day, he still doesn't understand what that means.

I had been privy to a lot of conversations with other general managers and other baseball people throughout my time with the Phillies, and the Chicago Cubs just were not on the right track at that time. When I finally decided to go to Chicago—which in itself was a little bit of a tough time for me because I had grown up in Philadelphia and had been part of the Phillies family for over 25 years, and I didn't really have to leave—it was such a wonderful opportunity to take an organization that was really not well respected, certainly not successful, and try to do something that I've been doing in baseball for years which is trying to fix things. I love to try to put programs together to make things better, and I just wanted to see if I could do it in a bigger framework.

So, I went to Chicago with guns blazing and big mouth blazing about what I intended to do. When I first went there, everybody talked about time frames. I told them I have no time frames. I want results rather quickly, and I want to make things happen quickly. I felt that because of where the Cubs were, we could make changes rather quickly because I didn't feel that whatever I did could hurt it. We knew that we had to win, obviously, on the field to gain that respect, but we wanted to start internally with our organization to make them understand that they were a very key part of what we were going to try to do in Chicago.

I was the first one to start yelling about lights. Wrigley Field was an old ballpark and we recognized that, but it was also dirty. We were determined to change those kind of things to at least make a good presentation to our fans—to make the fans want to come to the ballpark and recognize that even though it was old, it was well taken care of, and well respected, and clean, and kind of a family thing. It wasn't hard to do the family thing because that's what Wrigley Field is built on anyway.

I wanted the people to understand that we had to become people-friendly, that we had to become fan-friendly, and that we had to get back on track in terms of our work ethic, and that what we did as internal people in the organization was going to reflect on the entire organization. We made an awful lot of changes personnel-wise, which did not sit well with the old guard. But I felt that we had to gather people together that understood the direction we wanted to go in and had the work ethic that I was interested in.

We ruffled a lot of feathers. What we came out with was "Building a New Tradition." The media jumped on it, the fans jumped on it because we weren't winning on the field but what they forgot to read was the first word: "building." When you start building something, it doesn't automatically happen overnight. They said, "Yeah, new tradition, new tradition, not a big deal. It's the same old tradition—we're losing, and we're lousy, and we're not doing well." We knew this was going to take some time to kick in.

I was fortunate that I surrounded myself with good baseball people. I don't think Gordon Goldsberry gets enough credit for what happened in Chicago. I think he did a tremendous job in reorganizing and bringing the scouting department into the kind of work ethic that we wanted and the kind of evaluation that we wanted. The fruits of his efforts are still playing in Chicago and throughout the major leagues. Gordy and I were very close; and John Cox, and Charlie Fox, and Hugh Alexander all contributed heavily in finally starting to move toward gathering some baseball players who knew how to play the game and knew what winning baseball was all about.

We hated to lose and we didn't want to accept mediocrity, yet we knew it was going to be a tough process, and that's where Lee Elia came in. I had worked very closely with him in Philadelphia. I knew he knew the kinds of disciplines that were necessary in the clubhouse and throughout the organization to start the trend toward where we wanted to go. Lee did what I think was a tremendous job in setting the tone, and setting the discipline, and demanding the kind of pride and character that we felt was important to wear a Cubs uniform and be part of the Cubs organization.

He got himself in trouble and we had to make a change, but what he did set the groundwork for future guys, and the rest of it started to come easy. My background was in scouting and development, but I gave the baton to Gordy and he did his thing.

We had been raised in Philadelphia to differentiate guys who could play first-division, championship baseball versus second-division kind of guys. I had been around the so-called gamers as a result of my 1980 and '81 managing business with Philadelphia. Larry Bowa is the kind of guy I call a gamer. Ryne Sandberg, I knew from the minor leagues. I knew he had the heart, and pride, and gamesmanship to make himself a player and be a good player. Those kinds of people we felt we had to bring to Chicago because, to be honest with you, we couldn't find them anywhere in Chicago or throughout their minor league system. The only guy they gave us was Lee Smith, and Lee was obviously a super pitcher and a big part of our growing procedure. He was one of the old guard who made it—and a lot of them didn't. The guys that we kept insisting on in our trades and our talks were guys who had head and heart and could play the game of baseball the way we wanted it played.

Sut [Rick Sutcliffe]—you talk about a gamer. There's a man who exudes it. We were very fortunate to make that trade. Yeah, we had to give away Mr. Carter, but at the same time we won a championship that we would not have won if we did not have Sut. He brought to the pitching staff that professionalism and that great desire to excel and to win. All those guys that we got—Eckersley and all the different trades that we made—we basically thought about what kind of people are they inside. Not only their talent, but what can they bring to the table in terms of clubhouse, and rapport, and gamesmanship when it comes to tough times.

Sarge [Gary Matthews] is a perfect example. I knew Bobby Dernier and Sarge from the Phillies. Those were the kind of guys I wanted. Obviously they had pretty good baseball skills, but they had a comradeship and desire to excel that was special and important to us at the time.

To this day, I'm not sure what philosophical differences are. It really boiled down to, I guess, my big mouth getting myself in trouble again. And also it was the beginning of the interference by the Tribune Company into the baseball operations. When I went there, I was promised that we would have total control of the baseball operations.

As they learned the lingo and went to more and more meetings, they became more involved or wanted to be more involved in baseball decisions, and baseball personnel decisions, and baseball playing decisions. Even though I recognized that I had made several mistakes in some of my hirings—the Gene Michael thing was a big mistake, and some of the other things I had done could be considered big mistakes—but I always tried to overlook that kind of stuff.

I had reached the point where I was very satisfied with our growth. We knew the kids were just getting ready to kick in; Gordy's program had really just started to kick in. The Madduxes, the Palmeiros, Graces, Dunstons—all those guys were really just starting to blossom and come forward, and we knew within a year or so they were going to be major league people.

What I wanted to do was go down on the field myself and see if we couldn't generate some excitement and get things moving in the right direction in the clubhouse and on the field. The problem with that was there was somewhat of an insistence that a Tribune person come in and start running the baseball operations. I said, I can't have worked all this way and go down on the field and worry about whether this thing is getting handled upstairs. I said, Gordon Goldsberry is very capable of doing this. I said, Johnny Cox can be his second guy, and we can keep the flow of information and communication and what we've been trying to do on an even track, and we can go and do that.

They didn't seem to be satisfied to do that, so I backed out from being the manager and I said, "OK, I'll name Vuk [John Vukovich] the manager, and I'll come up and train anybody you want to bring in from the Tribune Company. When my time is over, the transition will be easy, and he'll be well trained in baseball operations, and we can go forward."

To this day, I assume that's where the philosophical differences became important to them. I'm sitting here and they're still wondering what happened to the Cubs.

We were just at the peak of finally gaining some help from our minor league system. I got there in 1981. We won in 1984. That was too quick. The fix wasn't done yet. The minor league system wasn't producing yet. But we knew it was close, and we knew it was coming. We had breakdowns in '85 and '86 that we couldn't filter in minor league guys quick enough, and we got hurt because of that. But we all knew that in the near future, things were going to be pretty darn good for the Cubs because of the talent that Gordy had gotten. There were no illusions of grandeur on my part.

I knew it was going to come to fruition and, obviously, we'd liked to have been a part of it. We left the Cubs in a heck of a lot better shape when we left than when we got there.

We had a grand old time with the lights. I was the first guy who dared say anything about it. And I was the first guy who dared say that's the reason the 1969 team lost. And that's the reason we lost in 1984, in my mind, because we lost the home field advantage because the television people wouldn't let us have that extra game.

The Cubs had to come into present-day baseball. We knew it was going to be a very difficult fight. I went to several different organizational meetings throughout the community and stood up and ranted and raved about what it would do for Chicago and what it would do for the Cubs fans. The neighborhood was pretty feisty at that time, and the city commissioners were thinking about their pieces of the pie. It took a lot longer to convince them than I thought it would.

I never wanted people to think I was a 100 percent night base-ball person because even though I was when I came to Chicago, I learned the charm, and the ambience, and the great feel that Wrigley Field and day baseball gives the fans. So, I never stopped saying that Wrigley Field and day baseball was special, but I recognized that if we were going to get into postseason play, it was going to become necessary.

I'm a fighter and I fight for what I believe in. That's just my nature. When I take a job, I sink my heart and soul into it. I think what people pay me for is my expertise and experience in base-ball, and I try to give them their dollar's worth. I thought it was pretty simple math in a way, and yet we had to battle through a lot of adversity to get the changeover from the losing and the acceptance of that, and the acceptance that good ol' Wrigley Field is going to be there forever, and wake up and recognize that if we're going to produce a winner and we're going to be part of winning that we hope to be, that we had to move into the next century, so to speak.

Ned Colletti

Ned Colletti started going to Cubs games when he was five years old. He estimates that he spent about 20 years in the bleachers watching about 400 contests at Wrigley Field before he finally went to work for the team. The Tribune Company had purchased the Cubs in June 1981, just a few days after the major league players went on strike, and then hired Dallas Green to be the general manager. Colletti took a job in public relations. Now an assistant general manager with the San Francisco Giants, he had a front row seat for the changeover.

Even though I had grown up in Chicago, I was working in Philadelphia covering the Philadelphia Flyers as a hockey writer. It's funny and kind of ironic, but I remember I was walking across the street and the newspaper office was across the street from Penn Station. They had a news bulletin from the *Philadelphia Bulletin* newspaper flashing on the newsline that Dallas Green was taking over the Cubs. I had been around Dallas. I thought, what a coup this is for the Cubs. Prior to Dallas's arrival they had some very, very lean years. The '81 team, if not for the strike, may have set a record for most losses in a season.

Dallas brought a totally different approach to the Cubs and to Chicago really. He's a big man in stature and has a big booming voice, and he really changed the culture of the Cubs. At first, I remember the fans didn't know how to take this guy. He blasted the old ballpark because it hadn't been taken care of. He said, "If you have an old house, it doesn't mean it has to be decrepit and run-down." He said, "We need to have lights," which was sacrilegious at that time. He really spoke his mind. He wasn't always politically correct or savvy, but he spoke from the heart.

Three years after he was there, he brought a division championship to the Cubs. I've got to believe that if Dallas Green would've been able to run the course and stay where he was in that company, I don't have any doubt that franchise would've won two world championships by now.

Don Grenesko

Don Grenesko joined the Cubs in February 1985 after serving four and a half years with the Tribune Company as treasurer. As executive vice president of business operations, he was responsible for directing all of the business and financial activities of the Cubs and negotiating player contracts. When asked about Andre Dawson's strange "blank check" contract, Grenesko deferred, saying, "That was Dallas." Grenesko stayed in the ballclub hierarchy for seven years before moving back into the Tribune Tower where he is now chief financial officer of Tribune Company.

We purchased the Cubs in '81, and we've had the philosophy at the Tribune Company of allowing each of our operations such as the Chicago Cubs to operate fairly autonomously. We've had kind of a decentralized operation structure. We go through a detailed planning process; we do that in the fall. Once that planning process has been approved, it's then up to the business unit to implement the plan. This is the philosophy we have with the *Chicago Tribune* and WGN-TV.

The Cubs weren't treated any differently than any of the other business units. We probably gave them more autonomy than other cases.

We don't have the seating capacity that we would like or the number of skyboxes or amenities, but at the same time the fans love Wrigley Field so they like coming out to the ballpark. So, you have to weigh that. We've tried to keep Wrigley Field the way it was as much as possible. We've shied away from doing the advertising on the scoreboard or on the walls and all that sort of stuff, and we took a tremendous amount of time and effort to make sure the lights and skyboxes blended in with the existing architecture.

I think we've tried to be fair in setting budgets. Everyone in the Tribune Tower is competitive and they want to win, but not at any cost, so you have to balance the payroll that you have for the major leaguers versus trying to make some type of return on the investment. I don't think it's really been a case of money. All of the general managers and managers have had the freedom to do what they wanted, and to form the club, and do all the trades, and develop the minor league systems and scouting systems as they see fit.

We would not have put a Tribune person in as general manager. There was never an attempt to put a suit in as general manager.

Lee Elia

*Lee Elia was handpicked by Dallas Green to manage the Cubs in 1982.
If not for some ill-chosen words, Elia would've managed the Cubs in 1984
when they won the National League East. He's been biting his lip ever
since. His response to reporters' questions after a difficult loss in April
1983 ended up costing him his job a few months later. Part of his infamous quote was, "Eighty-five percent of the people in this country work.
The other 15 percent come here and boo my players. They oughta go out
and get a fucking job and find out what it's like to go out and earn a fucking living." Elia consented to tell his side of the story about what he calls
the "so-called tirade," although he joked that he didn't want this interview recorded. That's what got him in trouble.*

We had won the world championships with the Phillies and went
into the mini play-offs in '81. Then Dallas went to Chicago, and
I was fortunate enough that he brought me with him to manage
the ballclub. We came from an operation that was home developed. A lot of those guys with the Phillies came up through the
program. It was a world championship ballclub. When we came
to Chicago, we had hoped we would get that done, and they did.
They got it done very fast.

I felt that one of the reasons Dallas brought me there was to
become a little bit more aggressive with things. We were blessed.
We had made a marvelous trade. We got a young man by the
name of Sandberg in that trade along with Bowa. In my heart, I
knew that Sandberg was going to be a second baseman who was
going to compete well. I never dreamed that he would become
quite the player he did become. I thought he'd be a very steady
ballplayer who would complement a good ballclub, a first-division
kind of ballplayer, but I never assumed the greatness that he would
arrive at in Chicago.

He came over as a second baseman, but we had made a trade
with Texas for Bump Wills and our third base situation was terri-

ble. We had a couple guys who were at the end of the road—my mind escapes me who they were now—but we thought for this given year we'd play Bump at second, and Bowa at short, and Sandberg at third, with Buckner at first. Sandberg started out very slowly. I took a lot of razzing about that. He didn't get his first hit until somewhere around the 26th of April. And they kept saying, "Why in the heck is this guy playing? Well, probably because he's from Philadelphia," and all that. The reality of it was that we knew he had to play through it—that was No. 1—and No. 2, whoever was the backup player was not nearly as good anyway. So, it was a catch-22. There was nothing I could do except play him and pray he'd get through it, and he did. Even in his rookie year, he hit something like .260, and scored 100 runs as a third baseman, and made a half a dozen errors at third base—or maybe a dozen, tops.

I told Dallas in August of the first year that "Sandberg will be your second baseman next year." He said, "If that's the way you want it, we'll do it that way," and we let Bump go. I knew in my heart, having seen Ryne in the minor leagues in Philadelphia, that he appeared to be stiff-handed, but he never missed a ball, and he was extremely fast, and he was a good student. He worked with Larry Bowa every morning at 8:00 in spring training endlessly. He's just a special guy. He's really a special guy.

The other joy that I had—you know, when you're not a name, a lot of the things that maybe you did do will never be recognized—I went upstairs and I told Dallas I didn't think Lee Smith was a starter.

He said, "He's started all the time."

I said, "I don't care. I think this guy has a chance to be a quality reliever."

So, we used him as a set-up man early to get his feet on the ground and now he's got more saves than anybody in the history of this game. That was another joy of mine.

The unfortunate thing about my tenure there was naturally in 1983, again being a very optimistic kind of guy and kind of aggressive—that's always been my nature. We started out slow. We knew we had a good bunch of offensive players. The pitching was suspect. We started out something like 3–9 or something, and who comes into town but the mighty Los Angeles Dodgers. They had just won a world championship the year before.

It was probably the inexperience of me understanding the magnitude of the media in Chicago—it spread out to so many different areas. After a given game on that dreaded day of the so-called tirade, the score was 1–1, I think. Lee Smith threw a wild pitch to allow the winning run to score, which was very unusual for the big guy to do that. It was a tough loss. To this day, I don't handle defeat very well.

We were coming off the field, and in those days we had to go down the left field line to get in the locker room, which made it even tougher at times. As we're walking down the field, Keith Moreland, our right field–catcher kind of guy, got into an argument with a fan, and the next thing I knew, Redhead's in the stands having an altercation. So, we had to pull him off this guy, and this is in a major league baseball game. We walked down a little farther after we pulled him off, and Bowa was by the tarp in the bullpen and somebody hit him in the back with something. He goes over the tarp and they're physically hitting each other. So, me and Vukovich, my dugout coach, we go pull him off.

So now we'd had these two things on top of a wild pitch by Lee Smith and I go into the clubhouse and had a quick five-minute thing with the club. I told them, "Hey, look, we got off slow, but we have a good bunch of people here and it's a long season." Then I walked into my office and it was packed with the mighty Dodger entourage, so to speak.

They were asking me questions, and they were not the kind of questions you should ask me after a tough loss. They were asking me about the Buckner–Ron Cey situation. Apparently, they weren't on the best of terms when they were on the Dodgers, and all the questions they were asking me I couldn't properly answer because I didn't know what they were like in the '70s. I was with Philadelphia.

But there were all these insinuations about the Phillies and the Dodgers and all that stuff. And I asked them, "Please, let's talk about the game." It was a tough loss and I'm still hot about going into the stands, and for some reason for that one moment—I never ever dreamed it would leave the locker room. Some fellow had a little tape recorder and he ran out of the locker room, and next thing I know it's on the radio, and now it's part of Chicago trivia. Who's the manager who said this and that?

I did say some things I really feel bad about. I think it's changed my personality. It kind of hurt me because I love players and I didn't think there was any place better in the world to be than Chicago. You'd be a damn fool not to think they're the greatest fans in the world. They've suffered through defeat and still love the players. But when I made my comments about the fans, I honest to God was directing them at those people who went after Moreland and Bowa. I didn't mean the Chicago people in general. That was something I often hoped they would always understand, but that was unfortunate.

The other thing that I said that was stupid was the Tribune had just bought the club, and I said, "Eighty-five percent of the people are at work, and the other 15 percent come out to this bandbox." Well, you know, that's the one I'll never get out of my belly. Why I would even say that—it just came out.

I think those statements finally did get me. Dallas called me up on the phone about 5:30, and I told him I had been a little aggressive with the media and he said, "Aggressive?" and I honest to God have no clue what I said. When I went upstairs, I sat down and listened to the tape, and I was stunned. He said, "I think we better have some kind of response to what you just said."

The thing that was really nice was the fellas rallied around me—I've always been a player's guy—and what has gotten wiped under the carpet is that we were in second place at the All-Star break three games out of first. We didn't have the household-name pitching staff. If you look back and talk about the ace of the pitching staff, it was Chuck Rainey and he won 12. He was the only one in double figures. There was Randy Martz and Fergie, and we were trying desperately to give him the joy of winning 300 at Wrigley. The only blessing we had was the beginning of a pretty good bullpen, but we could never get to the bullpen.

So, it was an unfortunate thing, it was a learning experience. There are so many beautiful and special things about Chicago. I'm going to be the guy who probably feels the strongest about the history of Chicago and the beauty of the town, and I'll never be equated that way. I'll always be the guy who said something about the Chicago fans and that's something I'll have to live with. That's all right.

I kept saying to Dallas, "If we can fortify our pitching," and sure enough, he went out and got six pitchers—Sutcliffe and Eckersley among others—and they went ahead and did it. They played good baseball in '84; the pitching was sound, and they had a great bullpen, and they win their division. I felt I was a part of that. Jimmy Frey was pretty kind to me. He said the other guy went through the trials and tribulations to get this thing here, and he kind of walked in and guided it to the end result. I thought that was nice of him to say. To this day, if I see those guys, it's "How you doing, Skip?" They knew that in my heart I was rooting for them to succeed.

Gary Matthews

He was the heart and soul of the '84 Cubs. Gary Matthews, a.k.a. Sarge, saluted his loyal left field fans and they responded in unison. General manager Dallas Green knew Matthews from their days together in Philadelphia and couldn't wait to get him in the Cubs lineup and, more important, in the clubhouse. Sarge hit .291 that magical season with 14 home runs, 82 runs batted in, and 17 stolen bases.

It was fun in '84 because the Cubs had actually never won. After being over there, even though they had a terrible spring, I remember saying, "Guys, we can win this." And they didn't really think so because of the way they'd played the year before and the way they had played in spring training. Our philosophy was to really think about your teammates, which meant you had to sacrifice stats. Consequently, we had six guys who drove in over 80 runs. Cey had an extremely good year that particular year, along with Jody Davis, Leon [Durham], our catalyst, obviously, Bob Dernier, who won his first Gold Glove out there in center field with the Cubs.

One of the things that we ended up doing was, because we played our games early, we put pressure on the opposition by winning early. Once they looked up on the board, because of the day games, and saw that the Cubs had won, there was instant pressure. That year, Keith Hernandez and I had a bet about which team would win and the guy who lost had to come and sit in the stands and look at the play-offs. Obviously, he lost that year in '84, but he returned the favor to me in '85 when we lost. And in '85, we had all our guys getting hurt.

Keith stayed with me at my place. So, he had to sit there. It was punishment to him. He was amazed coming in the clubhouse how guys were really rallying behind exactly what I was saying that year. I can honestly say—and I'm sure a lot of the guys would say—that that was the most fun year of all time. We made it fun. Guys couldn't wait to get to the ballpark to be able to take batting practice. I took a lot of pressure off say, even Sandberg, who would be up at the plate and he'd get a high inside fastball. I would be screaming at the pitcher from the dugout, and Ryno would have to step out of the batters box because he was laughing. Ultimately what it does is break the pitcher's concentration because he's looking over at me seeing who's screaming and yelling, and I'm staring right at him, and Sandberg, he's laughing, getting ready to go back out there and hit. Consequently, he had not his best year, but probably his all-around best year as far as having fun and going out to the ballpark and winning a lot of ballgames. We had a tremendous amount of fun.

I gave out hats, painter's caps, to the people in the left field bleachers, and you could flip up the bill and they said "Sarge" on the cap. Whenever I would do something good, the people in the left field stands would stand up, and when I saluted them they would sit down. We had a really fun time. It was really sad that all those people who were there during the season couldn't be there during the play-offs, because it's a small ballpark, so there were a lot of bigwigs who were there. It was one of my most enjoyable seasons.

Leadership is more or less God-given. I've always said the true athlete, whether he has better stats than anybody else on the team, your true best athlete on your team will make other players play better. For me, even in high school, coming up in Little League, it was the same thing. My mom always told me that I wasn't the MVP even though I might have had the best stats. I was more the captain, more the glue that held everybody together. When I would say, "Get 'em over, get 'em in"—I have tapes of me saying that even with the Giants as a rookie—to me, not to do that would be selfish. If I said, "Get 'em over," that meant when it came time for me to do it and I didn't, it wouldn't be right. We all did that that year. Consequently, we won. Not being able to get to the World Series takes a little bit away from it, but again it was a great year, and it was a great year for baseball.

One time, we won a game and I had brought in some softshell crabs. I had flown them in from Baltimore. They were calling me from the airport saying, "Get these things out of here." We ended up winning the ballgame, and the only one who was kind of irritated was Yosh Kawano because he had to clean it all up. There were spicy crabs all over the clubhouse with beer and stuff, and it was extra special because we had actually won that game.

We did a lot of things like that that year. After I did that, I got so many letters from a lot of restaurants in Chicago saying, "Don't order that from there. You can get them right here." It was just the little things to be able to bring the club together. We had a lot of fun. Fun comes when you're winning.

Dallas was the type, unlike a lot of managers and general managers today, who put the onus on the players, so if you made a mistake, he would blast you. If you didn't get the big hit, he would blast you. The players in my era when you did that, they would say, "Oh, I'm going to show you," and we'd go out and do better. Now, if you sit them, they say, "OK, fine, I'm going to take a vacation. I'll just collect my paycheck on the 1st and 15th." The pride factor, except for a handful of players, has left.

That '84 team really put Sut on the map. Sutcliffe wasn't coming over as far as a pitcher having great, great stuff. Prior to that year, they hadn't drawn two million either. I think that year, too, Cey had in his contract that if they got over a certain amount, he got a dime or something for every ticket. He made out like a bandit. It was just one of those years that was really fun. No one expected the Cubs to win at all.

Jody Davis

In June 1984, Jody Davis starred in a three-game series against St. Louis, hitting three home runs, including a grand-slam. Fans chanted the big catcher's name, "Jo-dee, Jo-dee" and he heard them. Davis cherished those moments. A workhorse, he shrugged off any suggestion that he wore out in the hot summer sun at Wrigley Field. Davis tied for the team lead with 24 home runs in 1983 and drove in 94 runs the next year, when the Cubs won the National League East title.

Honestly, the day games never bothered me. When I came out of the minor leagues, I came up with Chicago, so as a rookie you just got used to it and that's the way it was. In the eight years here, I never even thought about it. It was almost more of a hassle for me to go on the road, to change your schedule to that schedule. They didn't bother me. In fact, I kind of liked them when I was here. I would rather you get up and go to play. That's the mind-set that I had. That's the same thing when everybody kept asking me if I was catching too much. When I got up in the morning, I wanted to play. To get to play at 1:00 was just all the better to me.

The thing I remember the most about '84 was the way the whole 25-man team came together. There was nobody who had an attitude, there was nobody out there playing for themselves. It was 25 guys trying to win a game every day. That's a special thing when you can get a group together like that.

I couldn't say a favorite pitcher. Sut was so good in '84. As a team, we pretty much knew we were going to win that day. There were so many individual moments of the '84 season, and it was always somebody different. It was Sandberg's home runs off Sutter, and Sutcliffe wins 16 in a row, and Gary Matthews, the things he did, and Bob Dernier. Every day it was somebody different. When we got in losing streaks late in the season there, Steve Trout came up and won nearly every game he pitched. It was just 25 guys who had one goal in common and that was to try to win one game that day.

I heard 'em [chanting]. There's no way to not hear that. You can't imagine. It was great. It definitely got me fired up. You've got to relate to a crowd. When you get in a situation in a game, your concentration has to be at its highest level.

The one grand-slam I hit, they were walking Ron Cey intentionally ahead of me and they were chanting it while Ron Cey was still hitting. You got to hear that—you're on deck. It was just unbelievable.

I grew up 50 miles from Atlanta and the Braves and played two years for them, and still to this day I've never felt I was a Brave. I guess I'll go down as a Cub.

Lee Smith

*Only Lee Smith and longtime equipment manager Yosh Kawano know
the truth about whether Smith would sleep in the early innings of Cubs
games. After all, the slow-moving Smith knew he wouldn't be needed
until late in the game when it was a save situation. When Smith retired
in July 1997, he was baseball's all-time saves leader with 478. In his 17-
year major league career, which began in late 1980 with the Cubs, the
larger-than-life right-hander had 30 or more saves nine times. Four different teams wrote Smith off at various points in his career, including the
Cubs, who traded him to Boston in 1988 for pitchers Calvin Schiraldi
and Al Nipper. He wore uniforms for the Cubs, Boston Red Sox, St.
Louis Cardinals, New York Yankees, Baltimore Orioles, California
Angels, Cincinnati Reds, and Montreal Expos. Now, about those naps.*

I took my naps. I was dreaming about what I was going to throw
Mike Schmidt. I had to make sure I threw it right the first time. I
always relaxed in the game in the early innings. It was Yoshi's job
to get me up before the fifth and make sure I had on the right
"uni."

When I was with the Cubbies and I threw two innings, that
was like a day off for me. Now, guys complain if they throw more
than an inning. I think Rollie Fingers was the one guy who went
three innings more than anybody as a closer. He set the precedent
for closers. His saves were a lot tougher. When I threw, it was
mostly two innings, two and a third. Rollie went three innings in
a tie game. Most closers now don't even come into a game when
it's tied.

I only had one pitch and it was a fastball. I had the confidence
to throw it in any count. I think that made me a better pitcher.
Later on in my career, I had to come up with the forkball. I owe
an old Cubbie a plug—Frank DiPino taught me the forkball. I
think that added another five years to my career. My slider and
fastball, there wasn't that much difference between them. Frank

taught me the forkball when we were together in St. Louis. That helped me a lot. Hitters knew I had a good fastball and that off-speed pitch was one thing that helped me out in my career. Then I turned it around at the end of my career, because a lot of guys were looking for the breaking ball and I was throwing a fastball.

Throwing at Wrigley Field and Boston, the smaller ballparks, helped me because I had to make every pitch count. In St. Louis, you could throw a fastball 2–0, and a guy could hit it a ton, and it would go into center field. At Wrigley Field, you could make a good pitch and still get taken deep. I think that helped me with my control throughout my career.

I wasn't a media-type guy. I wasn't outspoken, or flashy, or anything like that. Nobody wanted to hear from me. I just did my job. How could you write a story about somebody who walks off the mound? I thanked God I got the job done and that's all that matters. I was sort of quiet. I didn't show up the hitters or anything like that. I just did my job.

Most of the people I remember are the guys on the grounds crew. All the ballparks I went to, I was really, really close to the grounds crew. I like simple people. I never did like guys who were impressed by what you did or how much money you had in the bank. I have some guys from the grounds crew from the Milwaukee Brewers who come to visit me to this day. When I went to St. Louis, the grounds crew from Boston came up to Montreal to visit me. It's just part of keeping things simple in life. That's how I like it.

Jim Frey

Jim Frey was the Cubs manager from 1984 to 1986 and led the team to the National League East title in '84. He moved into the front office as general manager from 1987 to 1991, and the Cubs won a division title in '89. As manager, Frey motivated Ryne Sandberg to become a power hitter in 1984. As the general manager, he traded Rafael Palmeiro to Texas for Mitch Williams in December 1988 in an eight-player deal. Does Frey regret trading Palmeiro? "Sure," he says. But let him explain why he made the move.

The thing that would lead me to talk to a young player is the fact that you've already established that this guy has talent, probably beyond what he even realizes himself. You're really working on his head. It's not the mechanics that you have to develop so much as trying to change a guy's mind-set. And I had talked to George Brett about the same thing in Kansas City before I went to Chicago. His reaction to my first conversation was exactly the same. When I said, "How come you're not more of a power hitter and not an MVP?" he said, "I'm not that type of player." When I said the same words to Sandberg, he said the same thing, "I'm not that type of player."

My job with Sandberg was to convince him that he could be that type of player. It wasn't so much physical ability as a state of mind and his approach to hitting. George had hit for a high average and led the league in hitting, but he never pictured himself as a big slugger, as the big guy, and I wanted him to be the big guy and Sandberg was the same way. A lot of people, even some of the top players, don't picture themselves as being a top player. It takes a while. They don't grow up with quite the confidence that people think they might have. With Sandberg, when I said that, his answer was the same as George. I talked to him about starting to think in those terms. I can remember when I first started talking to him, and taking extra batting practice with him, and getting him to hit out in front and hit for more power; some of the other players would tease him. They said, "Who's that wearing Sandberg's uniform?"

There were people in the organization who were taking the safety-first road, and they were worried I was going to ruin their good, young player. There were only a few of us who knew what was going on.

Sandberg doesn't talk. He's a good nodder. We had a relationship that many times was based on a remark or two that I would make, and he would nod his head and give me that little shit-eating smile and he would have a twinkle in his eyes. Even walking through the clubhouse sometimes I would just nod at him and he would smile.

What Dallas told someone else was that the reason he hired me to manage was that I told him I thought the team could win right away with a couple of changes. All the other guys he interviewed told him it might take a couple years. I always said I don't want to be part of a building program. That's a lot of bullshit. To me, it's a crutch. When he asked me, "What do you think of our team?" I said, "If you get a couple pitchers, we'll win." He liked that.

I'm not trying to act like I've got all the answers. I grew up always being on winning teams. When I went into professional baseball, my first year we finished fourth or fifth, and I couldn't understand it. That's the first time I'd ever been associated with a team that didn't win. Then I was on three straight winners in the minor leagues. After I quit playing, I went with the Orioles when they were the best team in baseball. I had been around a lot of winning. I got to the point that that's what you were supposed to do, and certain things you have to do, and certain ways that you want your players to act and perform. People that don't, they don't win. There's no secret.

I decided—for reasons I'm not going to talk about—I decided it was time to go. Stan Cook was very comfortable at that news conference with Larry Himes when he said that they were making a change. I had told them months ago I was going to go home. I told them I was going to fulfill my contract and then go home and retire. I decided I didn't want to put myself through the things that I was uncomfortable with. I said it's time for me to pack it in.

One of the things, when they forced me to fire Zimmer, I thought they had gone back on their promise to me when they hired me which was, "You run the baseball operation, we don't know anything about baseball." When they made me fire Zimmer, it was the first indication that maybe they'd gotten pretty smart. I'd been through those kind of things with other organizations, and I'd seen those things happen.

I loved being in Chicago. I loved managing. I liked the general manager job, but not as much as managing. It was different for me because I had never been out of uniform. There were parts of that job that I was never comfortable with. I went in there full bore, and it took me a year or two to really settle in. I think I did. We won a division while I was the general manager, and we drew two million people.

A lot of people say, I would never do anything different. They've got to be goddamn fools. What happened with the Palmeiro thing was we had decided that we were not going to have Lee Smith back, so then we had to go get a pitcher, a relief pitcher. We found out that we could get four or five players in that Texas deal, all of which helped us win the division championship. We then had Grace who had just come to the big leagues. We had Grace and Palmeiro, both first basemen, not a DH [designated hitter] league, neither one who could play the outfield, so we made a decision. It wasn't that we wanted to get rid of Palmeiro, it was that Texas wanted Palmeiro. At one point, I said, "Does it have to be Palmeiro?" and they wanted Palmeiro. So we decided we didn't want to give him up, but we did. Then we won, and nobody said a word until four years later when he hit 40 home runs.

The same thing with Lee Smith. That's what I'm trying to explain. It just depends on how you look at things, and how you're able to hang yourself out on the line or if you're going to play it safe. I wasn't too good about playing it safe.

We had a party at Dallas's house in spring training in '84, and he said, "What do we need to do to make this team win?", and I said, "Get a center fielder and a couple pitchers." We ended up getting [Tim] Stoddard, and Frazier, and Eck, and Sutcliffe, and he went out and made a couple big whopper trades. Now he gets calls, "Do you feel bad about trading Carter?"

All I read is that the Cubs don't try to win. Well, we won. When I got there we hadn't won in 39 years. They said they couldn't draw more than 1.7 million. Well, we won and drew two million. When we didn't win the World Series, I was the dumbest son of a bitch in the Midwest. In '89, it was the same thing. They didn't think it was a lack of talent or players with injuries, they said it was the manager which was the dumbest thing in the world.

It's just business. When you've got young men in positions where they're not terribly experienced and if they have some clout, they're going to say things and do things where they make mistakes. I don't blame anybody. I'm not mad at anybody. I said the nine years I was in Chicago were the best years of my career. I have great memories.

The Tribune Company treated me beautifully. I have absolutely no regrets. What happened was I had gotten to the point where I was 43 years on the road, and I had started to have some questions about whether I wanted to continue to live that lifestyle. I've heard some people say they want to die on home plate. Well, shit, I don't want to do that.

We spend a lot of time with our kids in the summer and take trips. You neglect a lot when you're gone for 43 years. I thought it was time for me to do something about it. [Stanton] Cook came to me before he made the decision on [Larry] Himes and asked me if I wanted a three-year extension. And I said, "No."

He said, "You're not going to walk away from this job."

And I said, "Watch me."

I just thought the time had come. The time had come for me to go home.

I've had a wonderful time.

Ryne Sandberg

*Ryne Sandberg epitomized consistency. He won nine consecutive Gold
Gloves from 1983 to 1991 with the Chicago Cubs, the most by any second baseman in the game. He also hit more home runs (282) than any
second baseman, including a pair of game-tying homers June 23, 1984,
against St. Louis reliever Bruce Sutter in one of the most thrilling games
in Cubs history. That year, the Cubs won the National League East,
and Sandberg was named the league's Most Valuable Player. Ten years
later, in June 1994, he unexpectedly "retired." Encouraged by his new
wife, Margaret, and his expanded family, Sandberg returned to play two
more seasons in Chicago in 1996 and 1997.*

Nineteen eighty-four was one of my most fun years. I was still a
young player at the time. It was my third year in the major leagues
and my first experience being in a pennant race and being on a
winning club. That was all new to me. I just showed up at the
ballpark every day, just having fun. I noticed the effect the club
was having on the city of Chicago and the fans. I thought it was
great. People were going crazy. It was a full house at Wrigley
Field every day. It wasn't that way in '82 or '83. In '84, the fans
liked the players that we had, and it worked both ways. It was just
a great summer all the way around.

Right in the middle of '84, on June 23, we were playing the
Cardinals. It was the backup game for the NBC-TV "Game of
the Week." The main game was rained out, so the whole country
saw this game. Tony Kubek and Bob Costas were the announcers.

They mention it to me every now and then when I see them that that game did a lot for them, too, as announcers.

The game was just going on like any other game, a lot of hits going on. We fell behind early. Willie McGee hit for the cycle and he kind of stood out early. I just remember Bruce Sutter coming in, and Larry Bowa told me to just look down and in against this guy, that's where his ball ends up, down and in. Sutter was one of the best relievers at the time. He came in to get three outs and the game would be over, and then I end up hitting a home run to tie it. Then I came up an inning later. I've seen a tape of the game. They had the credits going over the screen, and they named Willie McGee the player of the game. Right in the middle of the credits, Bob Costas goes, "Nuts, he's done it again and hit a home run again." It was just like a fairy tale game for me. It put us in first place for the first time that year, which we didn't give up the rest of the year.

I remember walking across and doing the Cardinals' postgame show, and I was answering these questions and in a lot of ways I was totally numb. I did that interview and then I walked back across and got a big cheer. A lot of Cubs fans were still there. I thought, man, this is great. Then I went inside and I could barely get to my locker because there were so many people to talk to. That was the start of my first experience with the media. It was pretty cool.

I wasn't used to that. It all kind of hit at once. It just snowballed the rest of that season. I was doing interviews at my house. The 10:00 news teams were in my house with the lights set up and all that, and they'd do their thing, and then I'd go to bed at 11:00. Then there were the interviews at the ballpark before batting practice, what with the season I was having and the way the Cubs were going. It was a new experience for me.

I drove to Wrigley Field with Rick Sutcliffe a couple of years. I drove with Jody Davis and Keith Moreland. The '84 team was special for that reason. Everybody got along, and it was a good bunch of guys. We'd sit and talk after the game and analyze the pitcher we were facing the next day, or talk about that game that day and just relax. It was a close group. When we were driving to the ballpark, first of all we'd check to see which way the wind was blowing. We had two or three flags we'd check every time when we drove down Irving Park Road. They were on some banks. As you got closer, then you really got an idea. We'd just check the flag and have a game plan.

Wrigley has that atmosphere. Old-time baseball. Thousands of players have been on that field, great players. There's such a tradition there, even going back to Babe Ruth. You get that feeling when you take the field there.

Second base was home for me. Once the game started, those were the best three hours of the day for me. Once I ran out and touched the base and was ready, that's when I felt comfortable. That's what I practiced doing, taking the ground balls and hitting. That's what I practiced and thought about, and that's what came natural to me, and that's when the fun began.

Sometime in the minor leagues or my early years, I was told to work equally at offense and defense. I think I did that. I think I spent my time on the field and took my ground balls, and made the plays, and turned double plays. Then it was time to go in and hit, and it was all hitting. I took hitting and extra hitting and did whatever I had to do. It was fun to do both well, to be an all-around player, be a good base runner—just be the full package. That's kind of what I worked at.

I had the same pregame routine every day. I felt I had to do that to be ready for that first ball that was hit. I didn't know if it was going to be right at me or way to my left or way to my right. This way, I was covered every day. It was like a comfort zone to be out there and take the ground balls, and after that I'd say, "OK, I'm ready for the game."

After I retired the first time, we made a couple trips to Wrigley Field in '95. I think it was the last series of the season against

Houston, and it came down to the last weekend of the season whether the Cubs were going to make the play-offs or not. It was just fun watching. I was going on 36 years old at the time and thought maybe it'd be nice to go back and play a couple more years.

At one point, we were watching the game and Margaret says, "You want to go back and play, don't you?"

I don't know if I was thinking that. I think I would've been thinking that a day or two, or maybe a week later. She caught it early. I said, "Yeah, I think I do."

It wasn't long after that that we called the Cubs and worked things out, and before I knew it, I was telling everybody I was coming back.

We were going to come back as a blended family and let Margaret experience that, and have all the kids experience that together, and do the whole thing for a couple years. It was very worthwhile. She loved it. She still loves it. I used to go to the family room after the games, and they had had a great time at the game. That's what it's all about. Winning isn't everything. It's pretty big as a player for the team, but for the fans and the families, they just had a great time coming to the games. They were entertained and they had fun. I think that kind of rubbed off on me—this is a fun game. I think players sometimes forget that.

If there was one thing that I would express to players now it's to have fun. It is a game, and they need to remember that every now and then. It is tough, and the grueling schedule and all that, but every now and then if they just remember you're supposed to be having fun out here and it doesn't last forever. It is a game. I'd like to tell them that.

Larry Bowa

The Phillies thought they got the best of the Cubs when they dealt Larry Bowa to Chicago for Ivan DeJesus on January 27, 1982. Cubs general manager Dallas Green wouldn't make the trade unless the Phillies threw in a young infielder named Ryne Sandberg. Fine, the Phillies said. Sandberg has his own chapter. Bowa helped solidify the Cubs infield and was a good mentor for Sandberg. The two spent endless hours honing their skills.

We worked a lot together. There are a lot of people out there who think Ryno happened to be a good player. He worked at his trade. When he first came over, they didn't know if he was going to play second, third—Dallas had him in center field for a couple games in spring training. Then we made a trade for Bump Wills, and then we got Ron Cey. So, Bump Wills played second, and Cey played third, and Ryno went out to center field at first. Then he went to third and obviously to second.

People don't realize that he was a good athlete. You can golf with him, he's outstanding, go bowling with him, you can play basketball. He was a natural athlete. Everyone called him The Natural because of how easy he made things look on the baseball field. He was a natural, but he worked at it. He was as big an instigator on our team as anybody, but he did it in a very quiet manner. Ryno's one of those guys, he didn't let too many people into his world, but once he got to know you, he was a lot of fun to be around.

In spring training, we were supposed to be there the 20th and we were there like the 5th. Him and I would go out and have somebody hit us ground balls, ground balls, ground balls. I think he had a good work ethic when he came to the Phillies, and he realized how hard it is and how important the work ethic was when we went to Chicago together. Even when I had retired and I came over with the Phillies, I'd watch him and his work ethic was the same. He'd take his ground balls, work on the double play, he'd work on bunting. He did everything. It was a matter of him just continuing his trade even though he was at the top of his profession. He continued to work hard, like he was trying to win a job.

Terry Francona

Terry Francona has a Bob Uecker–esque attitude toward his career. Francona spent only one season with the Cubs, batting a less-than-memorable .250 in 86 games in 1986, but he loved the experience. Fortunately for Francona, he can manage. He was Michael Jordan's skipper during the basketball great's foray into baseball in 1994, and was manager of the Philadelphia Phillies from 1997 through 2000. Here's a little insight into some of the Cubs locker room antics. Ryne Sandberg was known as a prankster, but he never got caught. Sarge was Gary Matthews, often a vision of sartorial splendor.

[Dennis] Eckersley was on one side and Sandberg was on the other of my locker, and Sarge would come in every morning all decked out. You know how he is. We had these director's chairs, and Sandberg would pull the stick out of Sarge's chair. And Sarge would come in all immaculate—you know how he carries himself—and he hit that chair and would go right to the floor and all hell would break loose. I would sit in my locker and laugh, and then we'd go out and get beat. But it would happen every day, and it was always great. Sarge would scream at everybody but Sandberg, because he was the little church mouse. That's what was so funny. It was hilarious.

We were so bad. We had all the same characters as '84, except it was '86 and '84 had worn off. We just weren't very good. Everything that went right in '84 went wrong in '86, and that's when I was there. That's probably one of the reasons things went wrong.

The worse we played, the more the fans supported us. I've never seen fans like that. The worse we played, the more they came. For fans to come out to Wrigley is an event. I don't know if the Cubs deserve it or not, but they've got a gold mine. People want to spend a nice summer day out at Wrigley. I would.

Leon Durham

He was known as Bull. Big, strong, and capable of crushing home runs into the Wrigley Field bleachers. Leon Durham played for the Chicago Cubs from 1981 to 1988, and was a star on the 1984 team that won the National League East division. He hit 23 homers and drove in 96 runs that year, the Cubs first in postseason play since 1945. But in Game 5 of the National League Championship Series against the San Diego Padres—a series the Cubs had led 2–0—a ground ball scooted between Durham's legs for an error, allowing the tying run to score. The Padres won the series 3–2.

I still have people come up to me talking about how great '84 was. There was a lot of love flowing through the city of Chicago. We had a lot of love for one another. That's where you have to start. You have to have some togetherness. You can't have one guy over in the corner, or another guy or two or three guys over here. You have to pull one another together. If you didn't have it today, then I'm going to have it today for you. We picked one another up, we complemented one another.

You never could have told me right to this day that we were going to go to a city and lose three games straight. I don't believe it happened to us that whole year, the way we dominated on offense and good defense. We had good pitching. I never thought we'd lose three games to San Diego. We didn't take anything for granted. We just got outplayed. We tip our hat to San Diego. They were the better team those three days. We got two games under our belts; we kicked their behinds in Chicago. Then they beat us. That's what happened.

I had a situation with a ground ball. I don't have to fade back too far as to what I did to help this ballclub win. I believe I played 140-something games that year; I had some aggressive power numbers. My average was good, my RBIs were good. But sometimes you have people who want to try to judge you on a certain play. It's a shame.

It happened. I had an incident with a ground ball. I can't recall the score, I can't recall the inning. We were up at the time. There was a runner on second because I was playing back. It was just a little squirreler hit to me by Tim Flannery, and it's a ball that I've caught thousands of times, but this particular ball stayed down and was coming at me like a snake. The best thing I could do was stay down on the ball. My foot was blocked trying to keep the ball from going there but evidently my glove never got there, the ball didn't come up. I can't recall if I ever touched it, or nipped it, or what. It was one of those crazy-type balls that came at you that you think would come up but never came up.

I haven't had any death threats. I haven't lost sleep over it. Of course, it's going to be with me as far as not going to the World Series, but knowing that play cost us the World Series—it didn't. I'm convinced of that. I haven't had to worry about, "Damn, if I could've caught that ground ball." What about the home run I hit in the game? I had five RBIs. Things like that. It's amazing in this game that the bad things stand out. Right to this day, Larry Bowa will tell me, "Man, you don't need to worry about that."

I'll say, "I'm not worried about it, but I'm kind of disappointed because overall we were a better team." They were going on and we were going home. That's the frustrating thing about it. No one was pointing any fingers. It was crazy how the situation occurred.

Then there was the Gatorade thing. Somehow, I don't know if somebody got angry, or somebody knocked the [Gatorade] bucket over, and my glove was just there and got wet. That glove was my sweetheart. I'm not going to trade my sweetheart in for something I use in batting practice. This glove was something I trusted in. I'm going to take my sweetheart with me. Maybe if there'd been enough sugar in the Gatorade, the ball would've gotten in my glove.

I don't put my ground ball in '84 on the same level as the Buckner deal. We still had innings to go. That was it for him. I think I still had a chance to maybe put the run back on the board. It wasn't for us, and I can accept that. If I had a problem with that, I wouldn't be in uniform today. I'd be somewhere hiding out. The love is there, and I want to spread it to other young ballplayers.

My mother thought I would be the minister in life. She thought I'd be a preacher. I don't know what I'd be doing [if I weren't playing baseball], but it would be something positive. It's the love. It's love. Man, when I stop loving the game, it's time for me to go. When you can teach something that you love, that you know this kid is going to follow up and be something and succeed in whatever they try to do. We may not get all of them, but we're going to touch some hearts. I love this game, and I'm going to give it 150 percent. I've dealt with the o-fer days, I've dealt with the successful days, I've dealt with going home and dealing with the family when I wasn't swinging well at the plate. That's part of the game. It matures you. Those things are what you spread on to the younger ballplayers. It's not always peaches and cream.

John Vukovich

Dallas Green brought John Vukovich in as a coach when he took over the Cubs for the 1982 season. Vukovich spent six years as a coach, handling duties at first, at third, and in the dugout. He also was interim manager for a day (June 13, 1986) between Jim Frey's and Gene Michael's tenures. After the '87 season, Green decided to go from the front office to the dugout to manage, with Vukovich staying as coach and being designated the skipper for 1989. That was plan A. The characters include Cubs executives Hugh Alexander and Salty Saltwell, traveling secretary Peter Durso, media relations director Ned Colletti, marketing director Jeff Odenwald, and Tribune executive John Madigan.

It all started with an interview in September. The first of November, Hugh Alexander called me and said, "We got that big son of a bitch talked into going down there to manage and you being his right-hand man and being the manager in '89. What do you think about that?" Hugh was Dallas's guy.

I said, "Well, how long did it take you to talk him into it?"

Hugh said, "About three weeks."

I said, "So, you want me to decide in 30 seconds? Call me back tomorrow."

Hugh called me back the next day and said, "What do you think?"

I said, "Tell you what, give me a two-year contract and put in my contract that I'm the manager in '89. Fine."

He said, "Goddamn, you're running a tough ship."

I said, "All I know is that in September, Dallas said a number of times that if we didn't turn it around in '88, he might be in jeopardy."

Hugh said, "I don't think he can do that."

I said, "I'll tell you what he can do is give me a two-year contract and make the second year a manager's salary."

"Damn, you're running a tough ship."

So, now, about two days later Dallas calls me at 7:00 at night and says, "Get in here tomorrow morning and bring a coat and tie. Don't bring those cowboy boots and jeans. Bring a coat and tie."

So I did. I went in the next morning and Durso picked me up at 9:00 at the airport. And I went to Wrigley and sat down with Dallas, and Dallas told me I was going to be the manager. We were in the middle of discussing the coaching staff and I knew I had to go downtown to meet John Madigan, so he says, "We'll continue when you come back."

I went down and met about an hour with Mr. Madigan, and came back to Wrigley and went back in the office, and I was in there about five minutes and Mr. Madigan walked in so I left. And I went to Colletti and Durso's office. About two minutes after I'm in there the phone rings and Colletti answers. Dallas says there's a press conference at 5:00.

I said, "Colletti, go and find out how many years I got." I didn't even know what I got in the contract.

So, Colletti went in and came back out after about 30 seconds and said, "Something's up. We're not calling this, the Tribune's calling this."

And just behind him walks Dallas and he says, "Let's go into Salty's office. I want to talk to you guys."

So, we went into Salty's office and Dallas, and Salty, and Durso, and Colletti, and myself are all in there. Dallas says, "I resigned."

I said, "Could we sign this contract before you resign?"

He said, "There's a press conference at 5:00. I want you to stick around."

I said, "Like hell. I'm gone. You just told me I'm the manager, and now you resign. I'm out of here."

As I was sneaking out of Wrigley, the camera crews were starting to come into Wrigley. I got out by the old marketing department by the old parking lot, and I was trying to find a cab to go to the airport.

Jeff Odenwald stuck his head out the door and said, "What the hell's going on?"

I said, "Dallas just resigned."

He said, "Where are you going?"

I said, "I'm getting out of here. I'm going home. I'm going to the airport."

He said, "I'm going that way. I'll give you a ride."

So I got a ride with him and we listened to the press conference on the way. I went home and I had a standing offer from the Phillies. I wasn't going to manage in Chicago, I could come home a coach and I took it.

So, I was coach, manager, unemployed, and hired in 12 hours.

Rick Sutcliffe

Rick Sutcliffe endeared himself forever to Cub fans in 1984. Acquired in a six-player deal that sent outfielder Joe Carter to Cleveland, the big red-head went 16–1 with a 2.69 earned run average in 20 games to help the Cubs win the National League East. In Game 1 of the National League Championship Series against San Diego, Sutcliffe allowed just two hits over seven shutout innings and had two hits himself, including a home run. He stayed in Chicago through the '91 season, winning 18 games in '87 and 16 in '89. Sut was Ryne Sandberg's carpool buddy. He tutored young Greg Maddux. He loved Don Zimmer, yet they constantly argued. He taught Mark Grace how to have fun. He warned Andre Dawson about Eric Show. A great storyteller, Sutcliffe shares a few insights into his days with the Cubs.

When I got over there to the Cubs, the waiver deal got messed up. Dallas had not cleared Joe Carter through waivers, so I had to wait four or five days before I could pitch. We had a meeting with Dallas, and my agent, Barry Axelrod, flew in with me, and Dallas just said—I think he was playing a game with me—he said, "Let's forget about signing this now. Let's wait a month or six weeks and see if you like us and we like you." Of course, six weeks later we met and I'd won 9 out of 10 and Dallas says, "We know we like you." I told him I'd like to wait. I remember that first week. We'd lost four in a row to Philadelphia. I said, maybe it's my fault because I was sitting around and couldn't pitch.

After the fourth loss, Lee Smith had thrown a sidearm curve to

Mike Schmidt and he hit it out of the park. Billy Connors called all the pitchers in for a meeting, and he went right down the line airing people out. He started out with Lee Smith. He said, "You're dropping down throwing sidearm curveballs to Mike Schmidt? You're trying to be cute. You got any mirrors in your house? You're not cute." And he goes down the line. When he got to me, I'm thinking, "There's nothing he can get on me about," and he starts screaming, "When are you going to do something around here? All you do is eat and shit around here." It's still one of the greatest meetings I've ever been involved in. He got his point across.

My wife, Robin, flew in for the Saturday day game against the Cards and that's when Ryno did his thing. It was a weekend crowd with the Cubs and Cards. We never had anything like that in Cleveland. After the game, as I came out she had tears in her eyes. She said, "Are all the games here like that?"

My first start at Wrigley was the following day after Ryno's deal. I said, "Oh, man, I got to follow this act?" I threw a shutout and had 14 strikeouts.

I don't think the city has ever had more fun during the regular season than Chicago did that summer of '84. The thing about that team was that it never played a game on the road. We might not have hit in the bottom of the ninth, but we had more fans everywhere we went than the home team. I played in Los Angeles and saw the Big Red Machine come in. It wasn't the same. When we were in L.A., they're chanting, "Jody, Jody." Ryno comes up in the ninth and they're chanting, "M-V-P." If there's 20,000 fans in Pittsburgh, 15,000 of them are Cub fans. We always had the most people behind us.

I can remember after we clinched, guys like Randy Hundley and a bunch of the former Cubs being around and just saying thanks. "Now we're going to talk about '84 instead of '69." I remember a bunch of those guys saying that to us.

Then there was Grace's first week in the big leagues. It's raining, and he comes down and there's a sign that says the team is hitting in the cages. And Grace comes by me and I'm pitching that day. Grace saw that he's in the last group with me. He should've known better than to mess with me—nobody talked to me on the day I pitched. He says, "Hey, Sut, it says we're hitting in the cages. Where are the cages?"

I'm mad that he's talking to me, and my warped sense of humor takes over. I said, "You go up the stairs here and take a left, and go under the stands and just keep going. When you think you've gone too far, keep going. Eventually, you'll get to this Old Style sign, and there'll be an attendant. Just walk through the door."

So, he takes off, two bats, his helmet, spikes on, his name on his back.

When it's raining, the people are underneath on the concourse, too, so he's got to get through the people. The fans are saying, "Grace, what are you doing?"

He says, "I'm going to hit."

So, there he goes, click, click, click. He finally gets there and he walks through the stairs and goes around the corner, and he's face-to-face with Red Schoendienst.

He says, "Red, you still hitting?"

Red says, "Son, I don't know who got you, but somebody got you good. You're in the visiting players clubhouse."

So now, he's got to come all the way back. And the fans are like, "Grace, what are you doing?"

He says, "Oh, I just wanted to see a friend over there." Click, click, click—a little faster.

He finally gets back to the clubhouse. He says, "All right, Sut, that was a pretty good one. So, tell me, where are the cages?"

So, I'm going to send him up the other flight of stairs and tell him to take a right, and halfway through the directions, I burst out laughing. I was going to send him to Murphy's Bleachers, the bar.

If Zim had hair, it would've been red like mine. He's like a father to me. We're both opinionated. What made us so close was our desire to win. Sometimes that desire got us in trouble. We're emotional about what we think. Our relationship really got close when he was the manager. Managers aren't supposed to win games; they're not supposed to lose games for you. He won 25 games for us in '89, just the stuff he did.

The biggest story was right after the All-Star break. I pitched against the Dodgers and threw a complete game on Friday. I came back on Sunday because the bullpen was sore and threw two innings of relief to help that game, thinking I'd be off at the All-Star break. I wasn't named to the team, but that was because of Lasorda. I got a call to replace Mike Scott, who got hurt. The manager picks the pitchers, but when someone gets hurt, it's the commissioner or league president, and they picked me. I said, "No, I'm not going."

He said, "Everybody knows you deserve to be there."

So, I go and pitch an inning. It was at the All-Star Game when I knew I'd hurt myself again.

After that, I threw four or five games, and none were good. Zim calls me into the office, and he starts airing me out. He says, "I can call a better game than you."

I said, "If you think you can call a better game, you call it."

He didn't talk to me for four days. He didn't say a word. All of a sudden, we're in Shea Stadium and I'm in the trainer's room getting a pregame rub. Zim says, "Come into my office when you're done."

He says, "I ain't calling pitches."

I said, "Wait a minute. Four days ago, you're the smartest son of a bitch on earth."

He says, "You want me to call pitches? I'll call them."

Joe Girardi is catching. The first pitch of the game, Zim calls a change-up. I never throw a change-up on the first pitch—not even the first inning. I threw it, and everything went perfect. Three innings, nine up, nine down. We score a run in the fourth. In the fifth, they get a base hit, walk a guy, bunt single. Bases loaded, Darryl Strawberry, in his prime, at the plate.

Here comes Zim out to the mound and he gets out there, and Girardi pulls his mask up. Zim puts his hand over his mouth which means he's going to cuss. He put his hand over his mouth because he didn't want people to see that on TV. He says, "I've got one thing to say—you're on your own." And he walks back to the dugout. Joe and I are laughing. I heard that Harry said on the air, "Steve, I don't know what they're laughing about. This is a pretty tense situation." Strawberry pops up, and Kevin McReynolds hits into a double play.

Joe and I go back to the dugout, and I said, "Boys, we don't know if we're going to win or not, but we're on our own."

I rode the first year to the ballpark with Jody. Ryno and I lived within 100 feet of each other. I remember one thing about Ryno. He was so shy. When I had my shoulder surgery, the team was on the road, and they got back and all of a sudden there's a knock on the door. Robin says, "Rick, it's Ryno."

I said, "Ryno, what's up?"

He says, "Nothing."

I said, "Do you want to come in?"

And he says, "Sure."

I said, "You want a cup of coffee?"

He says, "Sure."

We talked about the team, and he drank his coffee and he left. I said to Robin, "I'm not positive what that was all about. I think he just wanted to see how I was doing. He just couldn't say it."

There'd be days when I'd say I'm not talking first, and there would be times when we'd go to the park and there was nothing said. He was just quiet.

I remember when Dawson offered that blank contract, I said I'd donate $100,000 to get him. Dallas sent me a letter and said, "You just worry about pitching, and I'll be the general manager of this club." I knew the only chance we had was to bring him over. It meant that much to me that I would do that. Every time I see Dawson he asks me for that money. I said I didn't say I'd pay him, but they could take $100,000 from my salary.

I remember the Show thing in '87. Andre had hit two homers the day before, and then he takes Show deep. Right as he's going up to put on his gloves for his next at bat, I went over to him. I'd never done this before, and I don't know why I did it. I said, "Hawk, I don't know what I'm saying here, but something tells me this guy is goofy."

He says, "I know what you're saying. I'm going to take a look at the first pitch."

When Show bounced the first pitch, a breaking pitch low and away, I said, "Oh no." If you really want to get somebody, you get them looking out over the plate. They'll think, "He just bounced one. He isn't going to hit me now." I knew what was coming.

I started walking up the steps of the dugout. Right as he started to throw, I could see it in his eyes that he wasn't looking at the glove. That's why I got there and hit him on top of the head. John Kruk got on top of me, and I said, "If you don't let go of me, it's going to be you."

And he said, "You can have him."

And Tony Gwynn was there, and I said, "Tony, that's my right fielder and you know what position you play."

He said, "You can have him."

I went over to Hawk and there was blood, and I said, "Man, are you all right?"

He looked up at me and I don't know whether the conversation we'd had just clicked, but that's when he took off after Show. There wasn't a man on earth that could've stopped him. Our guys were trying to hold him.

It cost Hawk 50. He only hit 49 homers that year.

There was really a bond on that team. Maddux was pitching that day, and they told Maddux before the game that if he didn't win, he was going to get sent back to the minors. It was the bottom of the fourth when that happened, and I told Maddux, "You need three outs to get the win. You get those three outs."

He said, "No, I'm going to hit the first guy."

I said, "No, you do that, and you're going to have to deal with me." I argued with him.

He went out there and he smoked Benito Santiago; he hit him as hard as a man can. They kicked him out, and they sent him to the minors. That tells you what that kid was made of. When he came back up, Dawson and Sandberg made sure they never took a day off when he pitched.

Joe Carter

Joe Carter was a 23-year-old outfielder on June 13, 1984, and playing for the Cubs' Triple-A team. He had appeared in just 23 games with the big league club the previous season and had nine hits in 51 at bats for a .176 average. Not very impressive. On that June day, Carter was dealt to the Cleveland Indians along with Mel Hall and Don Schulze for Rick Sutcliffe, George Frazier, and Ron Hassey. Carter was stunned. And then he went on to play 16 seasons, hitting 396 home runs and driving in 1,445 runs. Enough said.

It was the worst trade ever made. That and Lou Brock. No, actually, it was a pretty good deal for both sides. It was a better deal for me because it gave me a chance to play. I was kind of laboring in a bad situation. They were going for the pennant and hadn't won in a long time, so they put all their eggs in one basket. For one year, it looked pretty good. But in terms of longevity—a lot of things were said, I couldn't do this, I couldn't hit a major league fastball, and it didn't turn out that way.

I was shocked because it happened right before a doubleheader in my hometown of Oklahoma City. Jim Napier came up to me and said, "Hey, don't get hurt. You're going up to the big leagues."

And I said, "Great," because they were on the West Coast.

I said, "Who got hurt?"

He said, "No, you got traded."

I said, "Traded? To where?"

He said, "Cleveland."

I said, "Cleveland? Oh, man."

I went to the plate my first at bat, I took three pitches and didn't even swing the bat and struck out. I think I struck out every time. I never swung the bat. I was just stunned. Once I got to Oakland where the team was at, I thought, "Hey, this is my chance to prove myself. This is all I wanted."

Shawon Dunston

Any Cub fan who sat behind first base when Shawon Dunston was play-
ing had to watch the game or risk being the target of one of the shortstop's
wild throws. Dunston had a powerful arm, and it took time and some
acrobatic plays by first baseman Mark Grace to keep it under control. A
back injury before the 1992 season hindered Dunston, but he rallied in
1995 to bat .296 with 14 homers and 69 runs batted in. A two-time All-
Star, Dunston signed with San Francisco the next year, came back to the
Cubs in '97, but was then traded to Pittsburgh. No matter what uniform
he wore, he was still a Cub deep down inside. Dunston was encouraged
by the "Shawon-O-Meter," Mark Grace, and Don Zimmer, but was
discouraged whenever he had to face Nolan Ryan.

In '89, early May, I was coming to the parking lot and this man
has my batting average up, .177, on cardboard. I didn't think it was
funny, and I was going to say something to him. He says, "Come
here, I'm not trying to tease you or nothing about your average,
but if you sign this, your batting average will go up. And I'll keep
putting it up as it goes up. Only you and Harry Caray will sign
it."

I said, "OK, I'll try it."

That day, I think I got two hits and my average went up to
about .186. It kept going, and they were flashing it, and everybody was teasing me, "Look at your average, it's going up." And
I'm hitting .200, and it kept going up. Then Harry kept pointing
to it and told Arne Harris, "Point to the 'Shawon-O-Meter,'
point to the 'Shawon-O-Meter.'" And Harry kept saying every
time I went up, "Feed the meter, feed the meter." Everyone
caught on to it, and my average went up to .278.

They made shirts for the play-offs, and they made calculators
of the Shawon-O-Meter, and how to do it, and this and that. I
really appreciated it. I thanked him for it. His name was Dave.

Everyone has a Shawon-O-Meter, everyone caught on to it. Everybody says, "I'm the original one, I'm the original one," but I know who the original one was. But I sign everybody's. The original one is in the Smithsonian.

My first year, Grace wasn't there, it was Leon Durham. I was a thrower. I was never a flipper or a guy who was really smooth with the ball. I just gun it and sometimes it takes off. I did hit one person, and it was kind of sad. One day, I remember there was a base hit down the left field line, and I got the ball and I threw it toward home. I threw it past the catcher and it hit the screen. It's a good thing they had a screen. Then the next play, the same thing, down the line, and I got it and the fans are all screaming at the same time, "Don't throw it, don't throw it," and I held it and they gave me a standing ovation. That's a true story.

I made Grace a Gold Glover. I know that. Everybody else throws perfect. You catch my wild throws, and as hard as I throw, you've got to be really good. It's like Zim said, if you have the arm, use it. You have a gun with no bullets, it's no good. But if you have a gun and you have bullets, use it in the right way. I was afraid to throw, but Zim said, "You're not a flipper, so don't flip it. Everyone's jealous of you, they wish they had your arm. It's easy to have your arm and tone it down." And I toned it down.

Grace was my security blanket. Leon Durham was, too, but me and Grace played together the longest. The first day he came up was in 1988, May 2. There was a double play ball and Ryno flipped it to me, and I threw it right in the dirt, and Grace picked it so we turned the double play. So, we come in and to this day he says, "I did it on purpose."

And I said, "How could you do it on purpose? That's my error. That's not your error."

And to this day, he says, "I did it on purpose."

I think I had about 10 errors by May anyways, so I wasn't about to make an argument. He picked 'em and from that day on, he was my security blanket.

Ryno, he was different. He'd come into the locker room and say, "How you doing, Shawon?" because he'd locker right next to me. It was me, Ryno, Andre. The two quietest guys and me, I'm the loudest on the team. He says, "How you doing? You've got everything back to the pitcher, you've got every steal, and you've got every pop-up." And I said fine, because it helped my fielding average. So I got all the pop-ups, I got all the putouts, and it helped my fielding average. I said, "No problem, Ryno."

I was young and he said, "When you get a little older and after 10 years"—because they told me that me and Ryno would be together for 10 years, and after 10 years you never know what's going to happen—and Ryno said, "When you get a new second baseman, you tell him what to do."

And Ryno retired in '94 and Rey Sanchez went to second, and I said, "Rey, you got everything back to the pitcher and you got every steal," and it worked that way.

Then Ryno came back, and Rey said, "Did you tell Shawon that?"

And he said, "Yeah, and now I'm passing it to you."

Andre did help me. He helped me when nobody knew. When nobody was around, he would talk to me. He helped me in how he carried himself when he hit a home run, going around the bases and don't say nothing, go 4 for 4 and don't say nothing, go 0 for 4 and don't say nothing.

Ryno and Andre, they don't say nothing. The way they played the game, I played the game. Play hard and don't disrespect the umpire. They always played hard.

I know one game we were playing in St. Louis and a ground ball was hit to Ryno and it went through his legs, and I panicked. I said, "Damn, he missed that ball, and you know I'm going to miss the next one if they hit it to me." He missed it. So, then the next day, the same thing happened, and he missed another one and it went through his legs. So, we take the pitcher out and he comes over next to me and he says, "Shawon, what happened?"

I look at him, like, what are you talking to me for? I said, "I don't know. You missed it."

He said, "I'm not going to make another error this year." It was about 30, 40, 50 games into the season. He said, "I'm not going to make another error this year."

And he didn't.

Nolan Ryan was the most intimidating pitcher I ever faced. If everybody pitched like him, there wouldn't be no $15 million players, or $12 million, or $10 [million], or even $5 [million]. I was making $200,000 and Andre was making $2 million. He threw a couple balls at Andre's head, and he fouled it down the line and fouled it down the line, and then he hit a home run, and I said, "That's why he makes $2 million and I make $200,000." I was happy to make $200,000.

To face Nolan, that's a hard day at the job. He was so intimidating. The first game, everybody said, "Shawon, he's going to knock you down, so just be aware." He knocked me down. He had a curveball that comes like a fastball, and I'm batting, and I fell down to the ground. The umpire calls strike three, and I'm walking back, and I'm mad and moaning and groaning, and I put my helmet back in, and he's staring at me.

When I got my first hit off him, I got a base hit up the middle and I rounded first. I was happy, and I got back to first and Vuk said, "Go look at the third base coach for the sign." Nolan looked at me and I put my head down.

Vuk said, "Put your head up, and look for the sign."

And I said, "No, that's OK. I know they're bunting me over."

He was staring me down. He was intimidating.

I remember one game, it was '86, Gene Michael had taken over for Jim Frey and everybody thought Nolan Ryan was doctoring the ball. I'm up at bat and everybody's screaming, "Check the ball, check the ball," and I'm in the batters box and I'm not moving. Charlie Williams calls, "Time out, check the ball."

I said, "Don't check that ball. Don't move. Let's play."

He's staring at me.

I said, "Don't check that ball. Let's play."

I knew he was going to hit me. And he threw three straight fastballs outside, and I struck out looking, and I go back to the dugout, and Gene Michael said, "Why didn't you check the damn ball?"

I started cursing. I said, "That man don't care about me, I'm not checking no damn ball. Why don't you ask Andre or Ryno to check the damn ball? Don't ask me to check it. You don't care about me."

No player would check a ball. You couldn't swing hard on him. No, no, no. You get a good swing, and he'll wait for your next at bat and he'll tell you to hit this while you're on your back. He was so intimidating. I think every player who ever faced him has a Nolan Ryan story. He was the toughest pitcher I ever faced, and Dwight Gooden was the second.

Andre was so quiet and I was so loud. He was about eight years older than me. They say I kept him young. He kept having knee surgeries, and he never complained. I remember one day we were playing against the Astros, and we had a 10-run lead, and he dove for a ball and I panicked. I said, "Please Andre, don't dive."

He said, "You've got to play the game right. You don't want me to play, take me out."

I took that to heart. He never complained. He respected the game.

When you hit a home run off Nolan Ryan, he meets you at third base. But when Andre hit one, he stayed near the mound and waited for the ball. That impressed me a lot. That's respect.

Gene Michael

General manager Dallas Green told manager Gene Michael to act like he didn't know anything about the negotiations for Andre Dawson in 1987. That way, Michael couldn't leak any information to the media. Dawson ended up signing with the Cubs for $500,000 and provided Michael with one of the few highlights of his brief managing career with the Cubs. Michael avoided being fired when he quit September 7, 1987, with the team in fifth place at 68–68. He didn't want to talk about his relationship with Green.

Andre was just a delight to have around. He was a fantastic player for us. He'd come in and he'd hit a couple home runs, and I'd go up to him after the game and say, "Andre, I talked to the writers after the game, and I told them I worked with you a little bit before the game—you understand, right?" He'd laugh.

The other thing I remember about him is he didn't want any days off. He wanted to prove his knees were healthy. He wanted to hit as many home runs and be as productive a player as he could be to show he was healthy. He'd come to the ballpark and I'd tell him, "Look, I'm going to give you a day off tomorrow."

He'd say, "No, Skip, my knees are fine."

I said, "Believe me, when I start giving you off-days, it will help you in the long run. You'll feel stronger and stay stronger throughout the season. When I give you an off-day, you'll start hitting home runs."

So, I gave him an off-day and the next day, he didn't hit a home run. So, he didn't like it. A couple weeks later, I gave him another off-day and he came back and went 0 for 4 and he didn't like this at all. I said, "Andre, it's just a matter of time. You'll hit home runs. This will keep you stronger."

So, a couple weeks later, I give him another off-day, and now he was really angry about the off-day and didn't want to do it at all. He came back and he finally hit a home run, and then he thought it was OK. He hit a home run and went 1 for 4 or something like that. The next time out, I gave him an off-day a couple weeks later and he didn't do anything again, so he didn't like it again.

Finally, he hit another home run after an off-day. Now he's two for about six games off, and next time out he hits another home run and he didn't mind it so much.

I have no regrets, except not winning enough. We had a lot of players who were maybe a little bit on the downside. It was an enjoyable place. We lived downtown, I had my wife here, and we walked to all the beautiful restaurants and things downtown. This ballpark and the fans, there's nothing better than this. It's as good as it gets.

The Tribune Company didn't affect me. I never saw any signs of interference in any way. I thought there was always ample money. They've had some bad luck here in players, and signing players and expecting a little bit more than what they give them. I think the Tribune has been a fantastic owner.

Dallas had his reason for things. I had mine. I'm sorry it didn't work out better. It's a tremendous place to be, and I was thankful for that.

Andre Dawson

Andre Dawson was desperate to get out of Montreal after playing 10 seasons on the artificial turf there. Prior to the 1987 season, Dawson made the Cubs an incredible offer, a fill-in-the-blank contract. The Cubs didn't refuse. Dawson was a steal at $500,000. He paced the National League with 49 home runs and 137 runs batted in and won the Most Valuable Player Award—and the Cubs finished last. Dawson found joy in right field at Wrigley. And because of that, he'll probably be wearing a Cubs cap when he's elected to the Hall of Fame.

Dick Moss, who was my agent at the time, and I sat down, realizing that Montreal was probably going to be completely out of the picture. We tried to come up with a situation where we thought I would be most comfortable. It had to be in the National League and on a natural playing surface. Atlanta was one of the other choices because of the weather, obviously still in the National League, a grass surface, and it was closer to my home. Chicago was at the top of the list because I just enjoyed Wrigley Field, the atmosphere and all. I wanted to go there first because I wanted to get a feel for how receptive management was going to be with the kind of proposal we had.

At first, I felt uncomfortable with it because, you know, it can get to be a pretty embarrassing situation depending on what kind of numbers they throw out at you. But then I thought about it and I said, "Well, monetary issues are not a priority. I just want to enjoy the game again and make sure it's still fun for me." And then I thought about it, and I said, "Well, they can't come in too low because the media would attack in some way." After analyzing it for a short period, I said, "OK, let's go ahead and go with it."

Dallas felt fairly uncomfortable with the process because it had never been done before. He thought it was some sort of ploy on our part, some sort of trick, and he just really couldn't figure it out at the time. He elected to have the Cubs lawyers look it over and evaluate it before making a decision. I said, "I don't want to leave this floating around too long. I'd like to hear from you in the next 24 hours or so." Sure enough, he called back the following day with a proposal.

It was a blank contract. It had nothing. Nothing. We just said fill in the terms. Whatever you think I'm worth, just jot it down on the contract and we'll respond to it. I just knew I didn't want to get back to Montreal.

Sutcliffe offered $100,000 of his own money. He always said the check was in the mail. In all honesty, I think Sutcliffe, being the seasoned pro that he was, saw what possibly could be a potentially good situation for the organization. With him, it was always putting the personnel on the field who had the capabilities of winning. Even though they had youth at some of the outfield positions, I think he knew that if I could come in there, I could be a bargain for the ballclub, considering what was being offered.

You get an adrenaline rush when guys try to run on you. I've always said I could do things in this game—it's not just about hitting home runs to win the game. You can get a clutch hit late in the game, you can throw a guy out, so have pride in all aspects in the game and try not to be a player who shines in one particular area.

They didn't want me stealing bases because they didn't want me sliding. They wanted me to pick my spots if it was a crucial situation. The thinking was I was wanted in the lineup every day and not to do anything foolish that would cause any type of freakish injury. But I always said I play the game one way and that's all out. And if I can't play all out when I'm out there, I'd rather someone else was out there.

The year I won the MVP, I was in Wrigley Field for the announcement and Harry telephoned. I think he was out in California, in Palm Springs. And he telephoned, and he said, "I want you to go and have dinner on me at my restaurant tonight. Congratulations. You deserve it." I said thank you. Actually, I had other plans to go out in the suburbs to Bob Chinn's, but we decided we'll stay and go down to Harry's and have dinner. At the end of the dinner, the waiter comes up and he puts the check on the table, and he has these two glasses of champagne. He gives me the bill and he says, "Oh, by the way, here's a drink. It's on Harry." I thought that was kind of funny. My wife looked at me, and I looked at her and I said, "Oh, well." It kind of made my night actually.

In '89, Jose Martinez worked with Dwight Smith and Jerome Walton as far as preparing them defensively. My thing, sort of, was the mental approach, being in the big leagues, the type of adjustments you have to make, the way you go about playing the game, avoiding self-inflicted pressures, and just making the adjustment there from the minor leagues. That was a season where things just fell into place for us. We were winning ballgames we probably shouldn't have. Everything was sort of Cinderella for us. We came out day in, day out, and had a lot of fun. Dwight Smith was the comedian and Sandberg would get him going—guys just had a lot of fun. Because of all the young players we had, I think people looked at us as overachievers.

Walton tried to be fashionable and he'd get into his thing, and then Smitty would follow suit. He didn't want to be left out. Sosa really wasn't a dresser. I took Sammy out—I guess this was a year later—but I took Sammy out. We were in Montreal and I just told Sammy, "Here, go to this store, [see this guy that I know] and pick out a couple suits and tell him that I'll come down and I'll square off with him later on."

Anyways, the guy calls me and I said, "I'll see you the next day before we leave town."

And I go there and I have a $2,000 bill. I asked Sammy, "What happened?"

And he said, "Well, I pick the suit, but I pick the one I like."

I said, "For $2,000, you could get three or four suits."

And he said, "No. Silk. Very, very nice. I like it."

He was the only one I really tried to extend myself with because we played right next to each other, and we communicated and talked a lot, and I took a special liking toward him. I saw in Sammy the natural talent come out very early. He was to me a physical specimen and probably needed to work on his uncontrolled aggression at the plate, but he had the strong arm and he had the mechanics that probably needed a little seasoning, but I saw a lot of potential there.

I pretty much saw the writing on the wall once the sixth season was up and over with. When they brought Himes in, there wasn't really any communication. I was told by some front office staff that he felt intimidated because I was a little bit more respected than he was. I really didn't want to get into that, because my main concern was finishing my career in Chicago. A lot of things just started to happen that pretty much told me my playing days were numbered there. And once there were no negotiations that spring—he said he elected to do it later on. It was the year of expansion and we had a meeting, and he said he wasn't going to protect me.

Himes made an offer to Sandberg and to Maddux, and then he pulled Maddux's offer off the table. Sandberg gave him the ultimatum to sign during the spring or he would probably test the market. I tried to meet with him again at the midpoint of the season, and they weren't interested. There were other things that came up—he would come by and speak to other players in the locker room and just walk by me. A lot of the players picked up on it. They wanted to know what was up, and I really didn't have an answer.

I was a little bit more confused at the way things were happening. At the end of the season, they made an offer—I think an offer for me to basically turn down. To me it was more a media ploy. We went into the off-season with the original proposal they made, and there was no movement. It was a ridiculous 10-year proposal, something basically to keep me in the organization post-career. That wasn't a concern of mine at the time.

Nothing happened as a result of their initial proposal. They went into the off-season and during the winter meetings, they finally called my agent and wanted to know if I had given any more thought to what their original proposal was. We told them, no, not at all, and they said they would be calling a press conference the following day to announce that I probably wouldn't return to Chicago.

Himes wanted to move Sammy to right field and in my opinion, there weren't a lot of players who were in the organization who could step in and play right away. The ironic thing about it is that he signed two players to replace me, one who retired and the other one had a horrible year and they got rid of him. Willie Wilson and Candy Maldonado. Then they lost Maddux, too. I thought that was even more devastating than my situation. The people he went out to try to replace Maddux with were the same thing. One guy had a disastrous season, a starter who really didn't pitch right. I look at it as it's the game. You have a change in management, and they have their own ideas on how they want to form their ballclub. And I just said my time was up there. I just didn't fit in.

The only ties I have with Chicago are the fans and some of the media. The media treated me real well. I think, had it not been for that, I think I would've left Chicago feeling very bitter. But I realize those are situations that as a player you can't really control. I accomplished a lot of what I set out to do there, and most of it was to make sure the game was enjoyable, and the fans allowed that to happen.

Jamie Moyer

Left-hander Jamie Moyer made his big league and Cubs debut June 16, 1986, against Steve Carlton, giving up four earned runs on six hits over six and a third innings in a 7–5 Cubs win. The southpaw totaled 200 innings in '87 and '88, but was traded in the off-season to Texas along with Rafael Palmeiro and Drew Hall for Mitch Williams, Paul Kilgus, Steve Wilson, Curtis Wilkerson, and two minor leaguers. Shoulder problems hindered Moyer, who was released by St. Louis in October 1991 and then by the Cubs in March 1992. By 2000, he was one of the most consistent starters in the big leagues, starring on the Seattle Mariners. Moyer still has fond memories of Chicago.

Dave Martinez and I got called up together from Des Moines. That's a story in itself. We were in Omaha, finishing up a series. Jim Colborn was the pitching coach, and Larry Cox was our manager. I went out and got on the bus, and Jim came out to the bus and said, "Jamie, come here." You have to know Jim Colborn a little bit. Very dry humor, a different type of person, but a great guy. He looks at me with this question mark look on his face, and says, "Do you think you're ready to pitch in the big leagues?"

And I said, "I don't know. Do you?"

He said, "I don't know. Do you think you're ready to pitch in the big leagues?"

I said, "I don't know."

I'd been playing, total time at this point, two years in professional baseball.

He said, "Well, they want you there tomorrow."

And I said, "Yeah, right."

He says, "No, go talk to Larry. He wants to talk to you."

So I went back in the clubhouse and Larry says, "Yeah, they called you up and they want you there tomorrow." So now, my head is just spinning. He says, "By the way, they're going to call Dave up."

I think, what a coincidence. We were roommates, not only on the road, but in Des Moines together. So, we take a bus back to Des Moines and pack the apartment the whole night, and we had maybe an hour of sleep. We get up the next day, and the trainer says, "Don't worry, you'll have a ticket at the airport. Just go to the ticket counter, get your ticket, and get on the plane."

So, we go to the airport and no tickets. Fortunately, I had gotten the phone number of somebody in case we had a problem, so I called and they came out to the airport. They finally got the tickets, and we made the flight. Now, Dave's got all his baggage and I've got all my baggage, and we weren't smart enough to take two separate cabs. So, we tried to put everything in one cab. We had to tie the trunk down, the backseat was full, I'm in the front seat, we had bags in our laps. We pull up to Wrigley Field to the players' lot across from the firehouse, and we have all of our stuff and it's BP time. We were late, but it was the first flight we could get out. We walk up to the gate and they say, "What are you guys doing?"

"Can you tell us how to get in the clubhouse?"

"Well, I can't let you in."

"We were just called up from Des Moines."

"Well, who are you?"

"Dave Martinez and Jamie Moyer."

"Well, I can't let you in. Nobody said you could come in."

So, we finally talked our way in and unloaded the cab and just set our bags in the parking lot. We get inside and guys were out on the field. My locker was up toward Yosh's room, and I got dressed quick and went out on the field and didn't get much done. We went back in the clubhouse, and one of the first memories I have of being on the team was going out for the national anthem—I was late—and we had to be in the dugout at a certain time. So, I'm standing there, and I took my hat off and put it over my heart, and my hand is just quivering. And Leon Durham was standing beside me, and in the middle of the national anthem he goes, "Don't worry, kid. We've all been that way." It was just like a ton of bricks fell off my shoulders. That's a fond memory I have of him saying that. I was just so nervous—and rightly so. I think most people are when they come to the big leagues for the first time. I didn't know anybody, I never had been in a big city, never had been in a big league camp.

I don't recall the date, but I know it was my first start in Chicago against what I'll call my boyhood idol, Steve Carlton. I grew up outside Philadelphia, so I grew up watching the Phillies, not necessarily liking the Phillies. I didn't have a favorite baseball team as a young kid. I found it too boring to watch. I was hyperactive.

Actually, I was supposed to pitch two days before that, and then they moved me back one day, and that day I'm thinking, "Geez, if they move me back one more day, I'll pitch against Steve Carlton." And I went to the ballpark that day, and they said, "We're going to move you back one more day," and I'm like, wow. Now it's, "Oh boy, do I really want this?" It was a pretty neat situation. It was my first major league start, first time being in the major leagues. I had never been to Chicago, I had never been to Wrigley Field, and really had no expectations on getting to the big leagues. It all happened so quick. I don't think I grasped or understood where I was or what I was doing. Being able to pitch at Wrigley was pretty awesome, but also being able to pitch against my idol I think was the ultimate.

The first hitter I faced was one of the Roenicke brothers and I gave up a double, so I mean a lot of firsts start happening. I gave up a couple runs, we scored a couple runs, gave up a couple more runs, we scored a couple runs, and we went ahead, I came out of the game with a lead, and we held on and won the game, so it was a great day. I was able to have my first major league start and win it, and on the other side of the field beat Steve Carlton, so it was a very, very memorable day.

My mother saved the clippings. I don't know how many scrapbooks she has. Really, it's my life. Football, basketball, baseball—from being a little kid all the way up, even today. I think I probably don't appreciate it right now, but I know she's doing it. I think as I get older and get out of the game, I'm sure she's going to say, "All right, where do you want these scrapbooks?" I think it'll be neat to go through them with the kids and my wife and look at the pictures. "Daddy, look at you." That kind of thing. It's something I'll appreciate later on.

The key to pitching at Wrigley Field is pitching on the days when the wind's blowing in and keeping the ball on the ground. I'm sure the grass is still very thick. It's very difficult to hit the ball through the infield if the hitter hits the ball on the grass first. That's a big part of that ballpark. The thing I noticed, too, as I spent a little time there, I started watching teams come in and take batting practice, and everybody's trying to hit the ball out of the ballpark. I looked at that as an advantage because maybe they weren't necessarily altering their swings, but they were swinging harder to try to get under the ball to drive the ball out of the ballpark.

I think the biggest thing is, I've always believed I could pitch. I don't think I had the success that I would've liked to have had when I was here, but I was a young kid—and that's not an excuse, but I was feeling my way through it. After I had a couple years' experience, I believed that I could pitch. When the Cubs did release me the second time, they offered me a coaching job. I was 29 and felt I could coach the rest of my life, but I still believed that I could pitch. It's just being in the right situation and getting the right opportunities. Did I know I was going to get that? I did not know. But deep down, I really believed that I could still pitch and that's what kept me going.

Mitch Williams

Mitch Williams provided plenty of nail-biters during his brief two seasons with the Cubs. The hard-throwing left-hander, nicknamed the Wild Thing, kept fans on the edge of their seats beginning with his first game, Opening Day, April 4, 1989. Williams was called upon in the eighth inning to protect a 5–4 lead. He got out of the eighth and had to bat in the bottom of the inning. Williams then gave up three consecutive singles in the ninth before facing Philadelphia's Mike Schmidt, Chris James, and Mark Ryal. He struck out all three to protect the lead and finished that season with 36 saves.

Sure, I remember Opening Day. I came in in the eighth and got out of the eighth with a one-run lead. I had to bat in the bottom of the eighth in my first game in the National League, and I hadn't hit since I was 18 years old. Then I go back out in the ninth and the first three guys get broken-bat singles. And then I strike the next three guys out. Schmidt? Either he's going to beat you, or he'll get out.

My first year was good, but my second year, I tore a ligament in my knee and the team didn't do too well. Me and Zim got along really well. He knew what my capabilities were. He was really the first manager who let me go out there and do what I did. He knew I was going to get in trouble. He was the first one who gave me enough rope to hang myself with.

The trade to come to the Cubs, I was ecstatic about. I was happy about the trade to the Phillies at the time. Myself and Jim Frey didn't get along at all. The way the trade was handled was bad and all that. I was glad it was made. I wished they would've handled it better. I save 36 games, we win the division, then I tear ligaments in my knee, and the next year I'm given seven save opportunities. I was 7 for 7 and I didn't pitch. Frey told me two days before we break camp that I'm not getting traded, then we went to Chicago, and I move into my apartment and he trades me. I think it had more to do with Frey than it did with Zim.

The Wild Thing didn't bother me. I've been called a lot worse. There's all kind of things they could've called me. I just didn't want people confusing the nickname with who I was. Off the field, I don't consider myself wild in any way. Dick Pole wasn't real keen on it. They played the song twice in Wrigley and I blew two saves, and he had them stop.

I didn't think it was tough to pitch there. People make a big deal out of the wind blowing out. For the first two months of the season, you can't hit a ball out of there. It helps you as much as hurts you. I think it evens out. You just go out there and pitch, and they have to hit the ball solid.

Being a reliever was perfect for me. I couldn't sit for four days. If I was a starter, I'd weigh 400 pounds. I like coming to the ballpark with a chance to play every day.

Jimmy Farrell

For every Cubs home game since 1982, Jimmy Farrell has tended the umpires' clubhouse under the Wrigley Field seats. He takes the game ball out to the mound before the first pitch. He stands near the steps in the middle of the Cubs' dugout. He just missed getting hit by a flurry of bats hurled by an angry Andre Dawson, who was upset at umpire Joe West's call in a game at Wrigley Field in 1991. Farrell brings the umpires water during hot July games. He'll join the gag in which the unsuspecting batboy is sent looking for the key to the bullpen. And he's the one many of the players talk to when they need a gentle, sympathetic ear.

It's been almost 19 years now. Before they built the new clubhouse, the players would come in here a lot of times to watch the game on television to see how a guy was pitching and so on and so forth. They had a lot of fun doing that. Dickie Noles, and Steve Trout, and the whole gang, and Jerry Morales, and Billy Connors—they'd watch who was pitching, and they'd go back to the dugout and tell how the guy was pitching. It was a lot of fun. Billy Buckner used to come in and show me all the bruises he had from getting hit with the ball all the time. He'd come in and have a cup of coffee, and I'd have to give him a little shot in the arm, you know. He'd go back out. It was a lot of fun.

Now we got a little different crew. Now we got two American League guys and two National League umpires, so I'm meeting all these new fellas now. They love Wrigley Field when they see it. Day baseball, and that's another great thing for them. They bring their families down. It's a great place for them to come, great restaurants they can go to, the city in the evening, and so on. They enjoy Chicago, very much so.

I'll bring them water on a hot day if they need water, or they might forget their jackets, or it might start raining and you've got to go get their jackets, or they might forget their pen when they go out. You're there in case they need you. It's fun. I'm in the clubhouse here from 9:00 on. It's good to go out in the dugout in case they need you, get some fresh air. You can't go walking around, because if you go walking around people want to know something about somebody, how's this guy or that guy, so it's a little hiding place for me, too.

You do what you can do. They're all good guys. I haven't met a bad umpire since I've been here. We have a lot of fun over the years, like Joe West, for instance. At the All-Star Game one time—this is going back. The umpires tip me. They tip me pretty good. When I got home, I told my wife Eleanor what I had. So, Joe West sees her the next day, and he says, "Oh, Eleanor, did Jimmy buy you a fur coat with the money he made?" and he told her how much I made.

See, I cheated a little bit on Eleanor that time. A little bit, you know. She says, "Jimmy, Joe West told me you made such and such."

I said, "He's kidding you. You know how Joe is. He's kidding you."

So, Harry Wendelstedt is the crew chief at that time, and the next time they come in, I said, "Harry, you once told me that everything that's said in this clubhouse stays here. One of these umpires told my wife something he shouldn't have told."

And Harry said, "What?"

And so I told him.

Harry fined him $50 for that.

Lee Weyer, he was one of my favorites. He must have had a feeling he was going to die. He used to imitate voices a lot, and he called me and said, "Jimmy, this is a friend of Lee Weyer's. Lee Weyer just died of a heart attack."

I said, "Oh, no way. What happened?"

He had me going for about a minute, and then he said, "No, no, I'm alive, Jimmy. This is Lee, how you doing, Jimmy?"

He died a week later of a heart attack. He was playing basketball with Eddie Montague and his kids. It was sad. Over the years, you get to know these different fellas. We're all kind of close.

Oh, Joe West and Dawson? I remember that very well. At the time, Dawson's right by me and he's throwing bats on the field right over my head, and it's on television. My wife sees that, and she sees the bats flying over my head. I see Dawson the next day—they forget the next day—and I said, "Yeah, you got me on television. You almost hit me with those bats."

He said, "Yeah, Jimmy, I'm sorry."

He's a wonderful man, wonderful guy. Wonderful class guy.

And so is Don Baylor. I'd never met Don Baylor. I used to see him with other teams and stuff, so his first day here I went out and I brought the baseballs out, and I was down by the little steps there in the dugout, and he come out and put his arm around me and says, "Nice to meet you, Jimmy. I've heard a lot about you." I thought that was a class thing for him to do. Here I am, a little clubhouse guy and he came down, out of his way, to say hello. That was a class act. He's a great guy.

Sandberg, he was one of my favorites. I was in his book. I went to his wedding when he got married to Margaret in Arizona. When he went out signing books, he'd always take me with him. Him and I were very close. I was like a father image to him. He'd tell me his problems. He'd come in and we'd talk about different things, like when he lost his dad that time and he felt bad about that, and his divorce, he felt bad about that. A lot of things, he'd come in and we'd talk about them, and he'd feel a little better. Him and I were very close.

His wife, Margaret, she really changed him. Now she's got him hugging people. He would come in here when umpires had their daughters with them before he met Margaret and he wouldn't put his arm around them, he was so shy, when they took a picture of them. They'd say, "Put your arm around her, Ryne. Gee whiz." Mark Grace, he puts his arm around them. Mark is a different type of guy. He'll give them a kiss and everything. Sandberg was so shy. Then when he married Margaret, he sees my wife now and he gives her a big hug and a kiss, and he's very outgoing now. She had him upstairs in a skybox, and he's throwing out paper airplanes with his name on them to the fans. She's a big influence on him. She's a wonderful girl.

Sutcliffe, he was a good friend of mine. One time he was on a losing streak, so I got a little rabbit's foot and I put it on the mound, you know, with the baseball. And he comes out and he sees the rabbit's foot, and he picks it up and points to me, and he puts it in his back pocket, and he won. He won. I put a penny on the mound one time for Dickie Noles.

We had a lot of fun. One time in the dugout, I put a penny in Jody Davis's back pocket. And he went out and hit a home run that time, and he said, "I'm going to keep this penny forever." Eighty-four, that was a great gang. I know them all.

Greg Maddux

To highlight Greg Maddux's achievements is just too painful for Cub fans. In 1988, he was 15–3 by the All-Star Game. In '92, he won the Cy Young Award after winning 20 games and compiling a 2.18 earned run average. It was just a sign of things to come—with the Atlanta Braves. He wanted to stay in Chicago, but Cubs general manager Larry Himes wouldn't budge from his offer, so Maddux left via free agency after the '92 season. Himes signed starters Jose Guzman and Greg Hibbard and closer Randy Myers to try to make up for Maddux's absence. It wasn't enough.

I really think that with the money they were going to have to pay me to stay, they would rather have had three pitchers. They'd rather have three for the price of one. I think that's really what it boils down to. Rather than just say that and admit that, and maybe they changed their minds the last month of the season or six months before the season started—I don't know when they changed their minds or what their intentions were to begin with—I think what it boiled down to was they thought they'd be better off with three average to above-average pitchers than keeping me. The economics of the game, where they wanted their team payroll to be, were choices made by them, and they elected not to sign me. Rather than just come out and say that, they thought it would be better if they didn't. That's what happened.

They originally made me an offer that I accepted three days later. This was before my sixth year, after my fifth. They made the offer, I didn't accept it on the spot. I called back three days later and accepted the offer, but that wasn't good enough. Because I had turned it down on the spot, it was no longer available to me.

And then at the All-Star break, after I had made the All-Star team and was on my way to having another good year, they made me the exact same offer. And I think they knew I would turn it down. And I did. I turned that offer down. After the season, they made the exact same offer again. It never changed. The argument we had at the time was what my market value was. They said they were willing to pay me my market value, and I was willing to sign for a little less than my market value. But we didn't know what that was. The only way to find out what my market value was was to go through free agency. And once I talked to the Yankees and the Braves, then they no longer had any interest in signing me.

As soon as they signed Guzman, they said, "The offer we made you was yours until we signed another pitcher." I think they signed another pitcher the next morning like at 9:00.

I think really it was all a bunch of hogwash. I think what they wanted to do was they wanted to get three pitchers instead of one and they didn't say it. That's why it got ugly. That's where all the accusations came from on both sides, on my side and their side. Looking back on it, as much as I enjoyed playing in Chicago and as much as I enjoyed living there and being a Cub, the grass was greener on the other side. I never thought playing for another organization would be better than it was playing for Chicago. It was a blessing in disguise.

I'm glad I had an opportunity to come over here and not only play for the Braves, but play for Bobby Cox, and play for an organization that is run just the way the players would run it if they were running it. I think we do everything we need to do to be the best players we can be on the field and no more. And I think the work habits are better on the important things. Looking back, I'm glad it happened. At the time I was crushed. I'm glad it happened.

Larry Himes

When Larry Himes was the White Sox general manager, he traded popular Harold Baines, along with Fred Manrique, to Texas for Wilson Alvarez, Scott Fletcher, and an unproven outfielder named Sammy Sosa. Himes was named the Cubs general manager in November 1991 and dealt for Sosa again in March 1992 in exchange for George Bell. Sosa has achieved superstardom with the Cubs. Greg Maddux also might have done so in Chicago, but he left via free agency after the '92 season, signing with Atlanta for $28 million over five years. Himes is blamed for that.

I came to spring training in '92 to watch our team play and not only me, but the staff was watching George play left field. He just wasn't doing the job defensively for us. To me, in the National League, you have to be able to play both defense and offense. I thought we had a glaring weakness there.

I asked our staff about how they felt if I moved George, and no one was averse to moving George, and they didn't know what they'd get in return. I suggested Sammy, and some of the eyebrows went up. They weren't sure that was a comparable trade. You're trading a guy who was an unproven-type player who spent most of the last year in Triple-A for a guy who was the MVP of the American League and who hit .300 the year before with 25 home runs. George was really a professional hitter and a professional RBI man.

So, we got a little feedback from them and they weren't too high on it, and I went ahead and made some feelers. At the time, the White Sox were building off the team that I left them and were looking for a DH. They were looking around and I was getting copies of the *Sun-Times* and the *Tribune* sports pages every day, and they were saying they were looking for a DH to fit in with Frank and Robin. I gave them a call and asked if they were interested in George. And they were interested in George, and we started the process. I told them I wanted Sammy right off the bat.

He was the guy I wanted. I needed something with him. I had some names in the hat that they wouldn't give me, and I ended up with Ken Patterson.

The day that I made the deal with George, he was playing a spring training game for us in Mesa. I told Jimmy Lefebvre to take him out after the fourth inning. He forgot to take him out. There was a fly ball, and George tried to make a running catch down the left field foul line and missed it and twisted his ankle. I was in my office trailer when I got the news about the injury. I was so pissed off that I had to take a 30-minute calming walk down the canal in back of our complex.

I came back and met with Bart Johnson, the major league scout for the White Sox, and we took George to get him x-rayed and had doctors look at him at the hospital. I was on pins and needles hoping it was not a serious injury. All it turned out to be was a sprain. That's what it was. Bart and I placed a call to Ron Schueler, and the deal was made. They were happy, and I was happy.

When I called George in to tell him, he couldn't believe it. He said, "Who did I get traded for?"

I said, "Sammy Sosa."

He said, "Who?"

I said, "Sammy Sosa."

He was upset at the time.

I said, "You'll be able to go over there and help them more than you can help us."

They put him in the right place, which was a DH. He was a professional hitter and that's what he was.

To me, Sammy was a breath of fresh air for our organization. He had some enthusiasm and some energy. When he arrived, he came right over to me, and he told me he would never let me down and that he would make sure this trade was a good trade and make me proud of him. And he's done that. He also made the comment that leaving the White Sox was like getting out of jail. The trade was good for Sammy; it changed his whole life. He could stay in Chicago, and he was coming with someone who believed in his ability.

Sammy came over and he was a breath of fresh air to me. He put some energy into practice no matter if he was running the bases or taking batting practice. Our players looked at it, and he didn't fit in that mode that they wanted him to fit in, which they assumed was the Cub mode. Cool, complacent, comfortable Cub mode. We didn't have that with the White Sox. The White Sox had a lot of guys trying to prove themselves.

The Cubs had a number of veteran players who had been with the club before I arrived and felt they deserved some kind of special rights in the Cubs organization. They felt they were more important than the team, had nothing to prove, and were more concerned with their personal agendas than getting on board and accepting the changes that would improve our club. A few veteran players, our so-called stars, thought they were the Cubs. They thought they knew how to play, they thought they knew how to win, and what I saw was that they really didn't know much. But they did know how to undermine.

When I finally stepped down, someone asked me if I had something to change, what would it be? And I said it would've been a five-year contract instead of a three. They weren't in good shape when I took over, and they're not in good shape now. They haven't made a lot of progress. When I look at my period of time there, three years is ridiculous.

Maddux is one of the two best pitchers I ever had. Jack McDowell and Greg Maddux. Both were guys who were mentally tough pitchers, who wanted to go nine. Both never wanted to get out of the game, and both wanted to finish what they started. There wasn't any way I wanted Greg Maddux to leave the Chicago Cubs. I know I'm a good judge of talent. I could see Greg was a quality pitcher and a pitcher we needed.

My first free agent signing was during the winter of 1991. We met with and signed Mike Morgan to a three-year contract. The same day we signed Mike, who is a good friend of Greg's, we made an offer to Greg and his agent, Scott Boras. We made an offer of five years at $5 million a year, with all the trinkets that come with major contracts. This was the longest contract in terms of years any pitcher had ever received, and the most dollars any pitcher had ever been offered. The $25 million offer was the most in the history of the game for a pitcher, and they were looking for more money.

The offer was left with Greg and his agent to think about and get back to us. And then it was removed. It was determined that Greg and his agent were given sufficient time to respond, and the offer was then taken off the table.

At the All-Star Game, Ned Colletti and Dennis Homerin met with Scott Boras and made the same offer we had made during the winter. Scott said no and said that Greg had earned the right to test the free agent market.

I said I would meet with Scott myself and see what I could do with an additional $500,000 a year for five years. I made the offer without getting permission for the additional $500,000 per year add-on. Scott gave me the same answer he gave Ned and Dennis, and thought it was a good offer, but they would like to test the market.

I thought it was stupid to continue to bid against myself after he already has turned down the highest offer in the history of the game. On the other hand, why are they so stubborn not to accept it? All they had to do was say yes. Twenty-five million dollars plus $500,000 a year for five years guaranteed, and all he has to do is nod his head up and down. It's in the bank and he's a Cub.

Greg wanted to be a Cub. We couldn't get him to say yes. Scott said they wanted to go on a free agent tour when the season was over and test the market. Test the market for what? More money? Longer term? It baffles me to this day how he could turn down the money and terms he was offered and take a chance on hurting himself while pitching the rest of the season. Why would you go on a tour if Chicago is where you want to be? I don't understand. They said he earned it and he has that right. But why would he want to do it when I know he wanted to remain a Cub?

Greg had about 10 more starts and he won the Cy Young Award. After the season was over, we flew to Orange County in the Tribune jet, flew out there and met Boras and his accountant in a motel room at the Orange County airport. We felt it was important to do this in person and not over the phone. Dennis Homerin, and Stan Cook, and Ned Colletti went also. We met with Scott, and again I gave him our offer of $27.5 million for five years with all the other stuff. I told him it was the best offer in the history of the game for a pitcher and that I would not continue to bid against myself. "We have $27.5 million sitting on the table. Do you guys want it or not?"

They said, "We want to take the tour and test the market."

"So, your decision is you don't want it? I can't sit here waiting for you. If Greg is going to leave, I have to look out for the best interests of the club." I said, "I'm not going to bid against myself."

Before we flew out to Orange County, I had asked Scott to have Greg in the meeting room with us. I wanted Greg there. They said, "Greg is in Hawaii playing golf."

I said, "Maybe he could come over? This is an important meeting. Put him on the intercom. There are some things he needs to hear."

They said, "No, we're his representatives and he trusts us."

I said, "His friends are with the Cubs. Everything he's ever done has been with the Cubs. He knows Chicago. He's comfortable with Wrigley Field, his wife knows it, all his family knows it. Why would you want to leave? This is something I think he needs to hear. His locker is the same, the same guys around him. There's some value in that." When you're making $27.5 million, it should be worth more than another $500,000 you may get to be around the people you know and are comfortable with.

They said, "We're going to test the market and take the tour."

I said, "OK, but from this point on, when I leave here, my objective is to find pitchers. I've got to go out and find pitchers. I can't wait, and all of a sudden you go out and sign with somebody else. Where does that leave me?"

I thought the other thing that was coming up behind the scenes was that they were going to take my offer and shop my offer. This is what agents get paid to do. They were going to take my money and go to other teams and see if they could get a $30 million offer and then come back to me and use that offer to negotiate against me for more money. "I won't sign with the Yankees for $30 million, but I will sign with you if you match that offer." I was not going to let that happen. They kept saying, "Five for six." That was the market for Greg. Five years at $6 million a year.

I wasn't going to let them use me. Greg could've said no. He has power over his agent. He could've said, "I want to stay with the Cubs." It got down to where, at the winter meetings at Louisville, Boras was still out there hustling and shopping Greg and he found out there weren't any teams. There were only a couple teams who could afford him, and they did not want to match our offer.

I had just signed Randy Myers, Dan Plesac, Jose Guzman. That money was for him. That was his money. I had to spend it somewhere else to make sure we had some pitching. All Greg had to do was say yes. I wish that had happened.

I get off the plane in Chicago after returning from the winter meetings. I get an emergency telephone message from Scott Boras. He told me Greg really wanted to sign with the Cubs. I said, "I don't have any money." Looking back, maybe I should've gotten on the phone and asked the Tribune Company for more money. Maybe they would've said yes. I didn't think that was my position to go begging for money once I'd agreed on a budget. I just didn't do things that way.

Two hours before they announced him signing with Atlanta, Greg wanted to know if we could sign him. Greg had called Stan Cook earlier. I don't know what Stan said to Greg. I told Boras, "We don't have any money."

When Greg announced, he said that he signed with Atlanta because he always wanted to be with a winner. That was a dig at me and the Cubs for not signing him. He wanted to sign with the Cubs and was trying to sign with us up until the last minute. He could have been with the club he wanted to sign with if he would've only said yes.

To me, it went down to the same thing that is happening today. The greed element is paramount. The agents are trying to milk as much money as they can out of an organization and are not considering what is best for the guy. What the hell is the difference between $25 million and $26 million? You have your own feeling of comfort, and after you get so much money it comes down to, where do I want to play? Who do I want to play with? Does my wife like the city? But never more money. Those were important questions we never got a chance to ask Greg.

I wasn't going to allow my offer to be shopped around. We all went within the guidelines of the budget. That's what we had, and that's what we were going to spend. Today, the budget is much different than it was when I was there, by a tune of about $30 million, and the Tribune is much more accommodating. Under conditions today, we would've signed him easily.

If Greg would have signed with us, I feel we would have won the pennant in 1993, and things would have been much different for the Cubs. Of course, I said no, and I'm the villain. Today, I'd do the same thing because it's the right thing to do.

Mark Grace

Until he left reluctantly via free agency after the 2000 season, Mark Grace was the "go-to" guy in the Cubs clubhouse. He could assess the state of the game in a quick sound bite and back up his talk with superb play on the field. He had a golden glove, came through in the clutch, and loved playing for the Cubs. A career .300 hitter, he batted an incredible .647 against San Francisco in the 1989 National League Championship Series—only his second full season in the big leagues. He may be wearing a major league uniform, but he's just a kid on a schoolyard diamond, playing with his buddies.

I think my first at bat of the postseason in '89, facing Scotty Garrelts, I remember I had a 10- to 12-pitch at bat. I was fouling off balls, fouling off balls, fouling off balls. He was coming with his heat and I'm fouling and fouling. Finally, about the 12th pitch, I hit a home run. So, my first postseason at bat, I hit a home run. After having a great at bat like that, just battling, man, it just seemed like after that, the rest was easy. There were no butterflies anymore. It seemed like it didn't matter what they threw me.

I hate using that "in the zone" phrase, you know. It's what I call "locked in." What we say in baseball is, "You're locked in." It doesn't matter what they throw you—hard, soft, in, out, up, down—it doesn't matter what they throw you, you're going to hit it and you're going to hit it hard. And that was pretty much what was happening. They were throwing me their best splits and curves, and I was hitting them. Unfortunately, it wasn't enough, because Will Clark and his teammates outdid me and my teammates. They were all great games. We just couldn't quite pull it out. That was kind of tough.

The whole season of '98 was a little more fun than '89 because I had grown to appreciate more how difficult it is to get to the play-offs. Everybody in the game of baseball knew me after the '89 series, so it was good for my career, but I think the '98 season was a little more fun. We didn't have the Hall of Famers that we had in '89 in Maddux, Sandberg, and Dawson, but we had guys who have a chance—Beck and shithead Kerry Wood—so there were some really good players. The '89 team, you were so happy for Zimmer and you were so happy for Andre Dawson, and Ryno, and Sutcliffe—guys who worked so hard their whole career to get there and they did it. But in '98, it was the young guys' turn to be happy for me, so that's the difference.

Catching the final out of the wild card game? Better than sex. Better than sex. The feeling that went through me, it was a tingling type of numbness. If I had died that night, if I had stepped off a curb and gotten hit by a train or something that night, I'd have died a happy man. I've got a lot of great things. I've got a great family; I've got a great life. I love what I do, but I could've died that night and had no regrets whatsoever. Instead, I had to live through '99.

I'm a Cub. This is all I know. They drafted me in '85. There's a lot of loyalty there. I mean, they drafted me, they gave me the opportunity to play professionally, they gave me the opportunity to play in the big leagues, so I'm very loyal to the Tribune Company and the Chicago Cubs. Everything I have is because of them—the cars I drive, the homes I live in, the lifestyle that I have, being in this locker room—is all credited to them. I wish a lot more guys would look at it like that.

These are my brothers, these are my soldiers. I'm one of the captains now, I'm one of the guys. I've got Mom, and I've got Dad, and I've got my brother. I don't really have a big family. I've got no children, except these guys, like Kerry Wood, these are my children. I kind of look at it that way. This is my family. I've got a lot of love for the happiness that these guys bring me.

For some reason—I guess it's because I'm so full of shit, or maybe there's respect on the other end because I've played a long time and I've played at a quality level—there's that respect out there, and that's all you can ask for as a player. Have your opponents' respect and have your teammates' respect. I think I've got that.

There's so much pressure on GMs by the Chicago media to make moves. Heck, Jimmy Riggleman got to the point where he was almost letting the media manage the team in '99, and it was doomed for failure.

I'm not going to blame the media for anything. I think I've got a great relationship with the media in Chicago. But there's two or three 24-hour sports programs, there's three major newspapers in Chicago; it's a huge media city, like New York and Los Angeles. Well, it's different than Los Angeles because Chicagoans actually care about their sports.

You've got columnists constantly wanting somebody else, you've got sports radio guys constantly wanting somebody else. You hear that and you're asked that, but I don't think it's fueled by management. It's fueled by people sitting behind a desk or people writing stories, and that's fine. You know, freedom of the press.

A guy like me, unless you really know and understand the game of baseball, you can't get a sense of my value. If you're just a home runs, RBIs, and batting average person, if you're a triple-crown person—well, yeah, there are first basemen who are better than me. But if you look at a lot of different things, like runs scored, on-base percentage, doubles, runners in scoring position—what's he hitting?—defense, can he do the little things, can he get a bunt down, can he go to the mound and give an ass-chewing when he needs to give an ass-chewing—there's a lot of things that I bring to the table that maybe other first basemen don't.

Am I Mo Vaughn? Absolutely not. Am I Mark McGwire? Absolutely not. Carlos Delgado? I can name a lot of wonderful, terrific first basemen, and I'm not even in their league when it comes to power numbers. But I can do a lot of things that can help you win a baseball game.

Zimmer let me know who was boss right from the start. He wanted me to succeed. He didn't want me hanging with what he considered the wrong crowd. He didn't want me going out at night. He didn't want me hanging out with veteran guys. We had a ton of veteran guys. Me and Rafael were the only rookies, and Rafael wasn't really a rookie. Zim got wind of us going out—Sutcliffe, [Rich] Gossage, myself, Jim Sundberg, Scott Sanderson, a bunch of veteran guys. He got wind of it and called me into his office and just chewed my ass out. He said, "I don't want you hanging out with those guys" and all that. He told me, "If I ever find out you're hanging out with Sutcliffe or anybody like that, your ass is going to be in Des Moines faster than you can say 'Jackie Robinson.'"

So, I was a little bit dejected. I was pouting at my locker, and Sut comes over and says, "Hey, kid, what's going on?"

I said, "Sut, I'm not allowed to hang out with you anymore."

He's like, "What? That's bullshit. We're supposed to go out tomorrow night."

I said, "Zim told me I can't go."

He said, "That little fat, bald son of a bitch." And he storms up the stairs and starts screaming at him, and the next thing you know, they're both screaming at each other.

"Leave him alone, goddamn it."

"I'm the goddamn manager."

It was something.

The other Sutcliffe and Zimmer story is the one in Cincinnati. Sut's laboring out there and he gives up back-to-back home runs. [Barry] Larkin gets him and then [Paul] O'Neill gets him. And in Cincinnati, when you give up home runs, fireworks go off. Boom. So, Larkin hits one—boom, boom, boom, boom, boom. So, then O'Neill hits one—boom, boom, boom, boom, boom, boom. Now Eric Davis is coming up, and here comes Popeye out to the mound.

Sutcliffe says, "What the hell do you want, you fat son of a bitch? I know what the fuck's going on out here. I just gave up a couple home runs. What the fuck are you going to tell me?" He's pissed off.

And Zim looks at him and he says, "Sut, I know you got things taken care of out here. I'm just trying to give that guy doing the fireworks a little more time to reload."

It's on camera, too, and they see me laughing my ass off, and Sut actually grins, and right back to the dugout goes Zim. And that was the meeting. He was just trying to give that guy a little more time to reload. That's my favorite one.

Dutchie Caray

Harry Caray lived a full life, and his wife Dutchie got to share a large part of it. One of the highlights of her day was when Harry would return home after broadcasting a Cubs game and the two would go out to celebrate a win or commiserate with fans over a loss. Dutchie, Harry's third wife, was at his bedside after he suffered a stroke in 1987. He made a triumphant return to the WGN broadcast booth on May 19. Dutchie knew how much Harry was looking forward to the '98 season. It would have been his first with grandson Chip in the booth. But Harry fell at a Valentine's Day dinner and died a few days later.

When I first came to Chicago, I was just amazed at Cub fans. I thought they were probably the most enthusiastic, loyal fans I'd ever seen anywhere with any ballteam that I'd ever traveled around with Harry. The Cubs weren't ever a very good team except for a couple of years, and those were just absolutely fantastic.

Everyone says, "Are you a Cub fan?" Yes, I am. Of course, I'm a Cub fan. Before I married Harry, I was supporting five kids and I didn't have time to be any kind of sports fan. My kids played baseball. We were a baseball family, and we really liked the sport.

On his way out to the ballpark, Harry would say, "Oh, this is going to be a terrible game." Then he'd come home and say, "Those fans are just unbelievable." They really all loved Harry so much. They always stopped him and got his autograph, and he signed everything everybody gave him.

At night, it would be a whole different scenario. They'd be coming up to him and say, "Oh, Harry, we love you. What happened to the Cubs today?" And they'd go on, but they were never angry. They'd never get to the point where they'd say, "Oh, to hell with 'em. I'll never be a fan again."

They're an unusual breed, and they're all over the country. The fans around the ballpark, they're the real die-hard Cub fans. I don't think they'll ever be anything else. You see people who say, "Oh, when I was two years old, my dad brought me to the ballpark."

Harry would go off to the game and I'd think, "Oh boy, that poor guy. What is he going to do today?" He'd be down if they weren't playing well. And I'd turn on the TV, and he'd be up and talking. When he got to the ballpark, his whole attitude changed. He came across as if this was the best day of his life. I don't think he ever had a bad day when he was at the ballpark.

I think Harry will always be alive out there. It was Harry's personality. He was the one who made Cub fans even more devoted than they were.

Sammy Sosa

Sammy Sosa's best home run season with the Chicago White Sox was 1990 when he hit just 15 as he struggled under hitting coach Walt Hriniak. When Sosa joined the Cubs, he was relieved. He became rich on June 27, 1997, when Cubs chief executive officer Andy MacPhail announced he was giving Sosa a four-year, $42.5 million contract. Sosa earned his paycheck in 1998 when he won the National League's Most Valuable Player Award with 66 home runs and a league-leading 158 runs batted in. He followed that with a 63-homer season in '99.

When I was with the White Sox, I put pressure on myself. They were asking for too much too soon. They were asking for something I couldn't give at that moment. When you're young and you make it to the major leagues, coming from a different country, and you see the situation in the major leagues, you put pressure on yourself because you don't want anybody to send you down to Triple-A. You want to try to survive here.

You want to tell the coaches what to do. You don't agree with everything they say, but you have to do it. That was my situation with the White Sox. After a period of time, I just made sure that everything was the way I wanted. Hriniak put me in a different way, a different situation to hit, and I never felt comfortable the way he put me, the way he wanted, so that's why pretty much we never understood each other.

I always said to myself, "Yeah, I could hit." But I had to do what they want me to do because I don't have a choice. I always believed in myself that I could do it, but the way he made me hit and put my head down, I never felt comfortable. That's why I never produced the way I was supposed to produce with the White Sox.

After I got my contract, my first big contract, I told Andy MacPhail in spring training that no matter how much money was in that contract, I will play the same way. I will show people that I deserve it. The way I've been working so hard, no matter how much money was in that contract, I will still play the same way, still go out there and perform and play hard every day.

I had to make adjustments in my career. I had to change myself, my personal ways. My reaction to things is different now than it was a few years ago. I had to mature. I'm a little bit more disciplined now. Everybody changes for a reason. Myself, I had to go through a lot of tough situations.

You have to understand, in this game when you have success, you could be from Mexico, the Dominican, Haiti, any country. There is always going to be a comment, there's always going to be somebody who doesn't want you to have success in your career. It's always going to be tough, there are always going to be people who criticize you. That's the way life is. You don't have any control over that.

When the people criticize me, I like it. That motivates me. That pushes me. That gives me more energy to do my job much better.

Jim Riggleman

Jim Riggleman had the longest tenure as Cubs manager (1995–1999) since Leo Durocher was the skipper from 1966 to 1972. The Cubs were 374–419 (.434) under Riggleman, including two 90-loss seasons in 1997 and 1999 which sandwiched a 90-win season and play-off spot as the wild card team in '98. He had the easy task of writing Sammy Sosa's name on the lineup card every day, and in '98, jotting down rookie pitcher Kerry Wood's every fifth day. And then Riggleman took the heat when Wood wasn't able to pitch.

To talk about '98, you've got to go back a little bit to '97. That was a miserable season. We got off to such a bad start, the 0–14 start. At the time, you didn't know it, but that 0–14 was against two of the best teams in baseball. At the end of the year, Atlanta and Florida were playing for the National League pennant.

As the season went on, we made some progress. A trade was made, and all of a sudden Mark Clark is on the ballclub and Lance Johnson. We lose Turk Wendell, but the contract of Mel Rojas was moved in that trade, and Brian McRae went to the Mets. Clark threw well the rest of the '97 season. [Kevin] Tapani came back from his hand operation, and nobody knew if he'd ever pitch again and he ends up 9–3. So, we see on the horizon this kid Kerry Wood, who may be there in the near future, and we've got Steve Trachsel. We look toward '98 as maybe things will be OK.

We go into that winter and put some other pieces together: [Jeff] Blauser, [Mickey] Morandini up the middle. Henry Rodriguez. We still had Scott Servais, a solid pro behind the plate. We felt in spring training that this was the best group we'd had since we'd been here, meaning Andy MacPhail's regime. So, we went into '98 with somewhat of an upbeat feeling in spring training. I know I was on the last year of my contract. Everybody felt there was some urgency, and I think that makes people raise their level of play, and the motivational skills may be working better for the manager and coaches when there's a carrot there that you've got to produce. And everybody did.

I think in '98, we played as close as any team I've been associated with to its potential as we could. We won 90 ballgames that year. It's not easy to win 90 ballgames. We certainly never threatened 100 like some of the great teams do. We won 90 with a group that was put together from a lot of different places. Glenallen Hill was added in the middle of the season, Orlando Merced, Gary Gaetti. These people came in and fit in so well to what was already a good atmosphere, and it just really propelled us into the play-offs.

The most obvious thing that carried us was the phenomenon that was Sammy Sosa. He was unbelievable. What he did was not only hit all these home runs that were winning ballgames and always making us feel like we could win the ballgames, but so much of the attention was on Sammy that it allowed other people to just go to work. Sammy had a huge media responsibility and requests every day. He handled it with a smile on his face and got his work in. People kept saying, "Don't you think this is going to affect Sammy?" And I'd say, "Well, look at what he's doing."

Kevin Tapani won 19 ballgames. His locker was right across from Sammy's. And he was able to go to work, put his time in, pitch his ballgames, answer a few questions, and get out of there. When Sammy would walk into the room, everything gravitated toward him. Everybody else was allowed to move in and out, listen to the music, stay if they wanted, and focus on the job at hand.

If Sammy had said, "I'm not going to deal with the press anymore" and hid in the training room or hid in the food room, then all that media contingent would have had to take everybody else's time. Sammy took a huge load off everybody there. It wasn't a distraction for Sammy. He hit 66 home runs.

I'm not impressed with how far the home runs go or how many. I'm impressed with when they hit them and the significance of them. He hit so many big home runs that year. In San Diego one night—San Diego had a good team, they went to the

World Series that year and we beat them three out of four late in the year in very big ballgames—Sammy had six RBI and a grand-slam off a hard thrower in [Brian] Boehringer late in the game. We won the game 6–4, and he had six RBI. He was having that type of year.

When we had all those great games with Milwaukee, no matter who was winning or what the difference in the score was, the team kept coming back and Sammy was always the catalyst in those games. He hit home runs that got us back in the game, home runs that tied the game, that won them in the ninth.

I talked to Sammy every day, but it was more, "How ya doing, big guy?" Just to let him know that I appreciated what he was doing. I never once had one conversation with Sammy about hitting, about his hands, his stance. Every now and then, if he was struggling or something, I'd remind him, "Hey, you've always hit, you're going to hit," and just give him a mental boost. That was Jeff Pentland's area. You know, too many chefs spoil the broth.

Sammy and I, I think, developed a real mutual respect. He knew I'd get on him. Sammy told me early on when I met him that he felt people were afraid of him. He was a big, imposing guy and had star ability as early as '94 and '95. He told me that, "Sometimes people don't want to say anything to me, like they're afraid of me." What he was saying was, "If you see me doing something, let me know." And I'd do that. If I didn't like something he did on the bases or whatever, I'd talk to him.

At the end, I didn't know I was fired yet and Sammy came in on the last day in St. Louis when we lost our last game of the season against the Cardinals, and he came in and shook my hand and said, "Thanks for everything." I think he knew I was getting fired. He probably knew. They probably told him before they told me, you know.

It sounds like a ridiculous thing to say, but Kerry's game had to be the greatest game anybody's ever pitched in Wrigley Field. I said this to a couple coaches the other day, "You know, one of the greatest games that ever has been pitched was Sandy Koufax's perfect game. Two people who were in that game, Billy Williams and Ron Santo, said Kerry Wood's performance was better." He struck out more, neither walked anybody. There was basically an off-the-end-of-the-bat ground ball, questionable hit—it was a hit—but we'd seen that play made, too. If that play's made and that is a perfect game, then that is the best game ever pitched. A 20-strikeout perfect game. Koufax struck out, what, 18 in his game? Fifteen? I don't know how you could throw a better ballgame than Wood did, and it was a 1–0 game.

Somewhere around the seventh or eighth innings, somebody said, "He's got 16 strikeouts or something." And at that point I said, "Damn, he's got that many?" I didn't know what the record was, and I don't think Kerry knew how many strikeouts he had or what the record was.

It's really a double-edged sword when you have a guy like Kerry Wood, or a young Nolan Ryan, or a young Koufax. It was the right time to bring Kerry to the big leagues. His performance proved that out. But you have to understand when you bring a young power pitcher to the big leagues, it's going to take a lot of pitches to get the job done. It's not going to be this Greg Maddux 92-pitch, eight-inning performance. So, you have to say, "Are we willing to let this guy do this, or are we going to baby-sit him and pull him out after six or seven innings?" We chose the latter. I would pull him out after six, seven innings most of the time, and he'd have anywhere from 105 to 118 pitches. When he dominated the games and he got 125, 130 pitches, I didn't like that, but we were trying to win the game, too. It's a tremendous, uplifting situation for the other dugout when you pull a Randy Johnson out of the game or when you pull Kerry Wood out of the game.

When you send him out there and he gets to 122 pitches, you've got a hitter there, two outs, you think, "The guy can't hit him." So, throw one over the plate, pop it up, and next thing you know, it's 3–2, three foul balls, and the infielder misses a ball. Now he's thrown 130 pitches, and you're starting to go, "Oh, God."

There is an occasion where you have this young pitcher out there, he's going to have to throw 130 pitches sometimes. And he's in a pennant race.

You make a decision to have this young player on the club, and from upstairs, Andy and Ed were very supportive of that, and they were saying, "Hey, let him pitch." I pulled him out of games at the irritation of the fans and the media. Ed and Andy at times probably felt like, "Damn, I thought he could've gone a little more." I thought I handled him the right way. I caught a lot of grief over it.

And then when he came up hurt the next year, a lot of people were saying, "See, he averaged this many pitches last year, that's too many for a young kid." People turned the tables on me a little bit. It's the nature of throwing the ball. Kerry Wood's arm was hurt since high school. That arm was going to go. I don't care if he threw 50 pitches, 70 pitches, 100 pitches, 200 pitches. I think, looking back on it, Kerry wouldn't have it any other way. He experienced a great '98 season. He helped the club get in the play-offs, he pitched in the play-offs. What was inevitable to happen did happen, and he got it fixed and he's fine.

To talk about '99, you have to talk about '98 a little. Gary Gaetti got us in the play-offs. Mickey Morandini got us in the play-offs. Glenallen Hill got us in the play-offs. So, you've got to make decisions now. Do you bring those people back? When we struggled in '99, everybody said, "How could you bring those people back?" Well, how do you not bring them back? If you have any compassion, any blood in your veins, any feeling about your players, how do you call Gary Gaetti and say, "We don't want you back"? He was unbelievable for us. I'm not smart enough to know that this guy who hit .325 from August to September and is five months older is now going to hit .201. Who knows that?

Mickey Morandini hit .296 in '98. I think Mickey's '99 season was affected by the fact that his agent turned down a contract extension in spring training, and that's got to wear on you a little bit. When you know you've just turned down a lot of money and now you're in a little slump, you might start pressing a little bit. "I've got to show them I'm worth that money."

Basically, people who we were counting on—Gaetti, Morandini, Blauser—they just didn't get off to a good '99. That's three out of eight who were struggling. Benito Santiago, who I personally begged for, struggled. So, there's four guys. Sammy and Mark Grace were doing the same thing they always did. We just had a lot of people struggling. Kerry broke down. Tapani was not near what he could be with back problems, and he came out of spring training with a sore shoulder. We were trying to do it with Andrew Lorraine, and Micah Bowie, and Kyle Farnsworth.

Everything that could go wrong went wrong. It just culminated into a repeat of '97, of this miserable situation, and nobody could see any light at the end of the tunnel.

Through that time, I'd go into the clubhouse after games and continue to try to be positive and motivate and remind the ballclub that we had to have some pride. "You're a professional. You signed a contract, you've got to honor the contract. You've got to give everything you have." I was constantly bringing up that two great players won MVPs on last-place ballclubs, Andre Dawson and Dale Murphy. They found a way to motivate themselves in miserable situations. It fell on deaf ears. When you lose as much as we did, it just starts to fall on deaf ears.

I've never doubted my abilities to manage, but I also know those hours when you're not actually managing that game—when the umpire says play ball, anybody can manage—it's those other hours. You're getting beaten down all the time, people who are close to you are worried, and it just kind of tears away at your fiber a little bit.

I got beat in San Diego a lot. I don't know the exact number of games I won in San Diego, but I would challenge anybody to win one more game than I did there. I don't care what some talk radio guy says about how horseshit my record was, nobody could've won another game.

You add that to my losses here in Chicago, and it starts eating away at your spirit. I don't think anybody could've won another game in my five years here. That doesn't mean I shouldn't be fired. That's the nature of it. Another voice needs to be heard. Jim Lefebvre was .500 the last year he was there and he got fired. For whatever reason, somebody said, "You know what? I've heard enough of him. I need somebody else."

Kerry Wood

The Cubs had to change their pitching charts in 1998 to accommodate Kerry Wood's 100 mile-per-hour pitches. In only his fifth major league start on May 6, the 20-year-old right-hander struck out 20 Houston Astros, tying a major league record set by a fellow Texas fireballer, Roger Clemens. Wood whiffed 233 in his first season en route to winning the National League Rookie of the Year Award. The sophomore jinx hit hard when he was forced to undergo elbow surgery in April 1999.

When I was growing up in Texas, there was never a lack of competition at every league, every level. Me, my family, my friends and their families—that's where you went. You were at the ballpark every day. Even on nights you weren't playing, you were at the ballpark. You were there, just checking out other teams, and just hanging out and having a good time.

Texas is a real big football state, and I played football when I was younger for a couple years, but it really wasn't my thing. I was a slow white guy, and I didn't have a lot of football talent. I figured I could stand up on a mound and throw a little ball easier than I could get away from people.

I'd pretend to be a hitter before I'd be a pitcher. I was Mc-Gwire, Canseco, those guys. When I was on the mound, I started by trying to emulate Nolan Ryan's mechanics and just went from there. I tried to have a little intimidation factor if possible. That didn't come until later in high school when I started throwing harder. I never tried to be a certain pitcher on the mound. I just tried to be myself.

I do everything hard. I try to throw hard, I try to swing hard. My golf game is terrible, but I swing hard. As I started getting into high school—I think it was my sophomore year—I realized I had a little better arm than the rest of the guys and was throwing a lot harder than the rest of the guys. As I grew, my arm strength got stronger and I was able to throw even harder.

The only pitching coach I ever had was my dad. He started me with my mechanics. I had pretty strong mechanics, even as a young pitcher. My mechanics never got messed with. They're still pretty much the same now as they were when I was younger. I never really had a pitching coach try to change my mechanics. The arm strength is just God-given, so you go from there.

I like strikeouts. They give you a little rush of adrenaline. And there's days when I want to go out and get 27 ground balls if I can. But the days you go out, and you feel good, and you have good stuff, and you go 0–1 or 0–2 on a hitter—those are good days. I was talking to one of my buddies who's a left-hander and not a strikeout pitcher, and I said, "When you get 0–1 on a hitter, what are you thinking?" And he said he never thinks about strikeouts, even when he's got two strikes on a guy. I go 0–1, I'm looking for a strikeout in those situations. And when I get two strikes on a guy, the majority of the time, I'm looking for a strikeout.

I've seen the film of the game against Houston. I can't believe it's me, just from the control standpoint. I've had days where I've gone out with that kind of stuff, but because of the pitch count or I've walked a couple guys, I never finish the game. I've had that kind of stuff before, but I wasn't able to finish. I'd be done in the sixth or seventh because of the pitch count or going full count to a lot of guys. It's just that day, that particular day, I was getting the calls, I was getting some breaks. A lot of luck was on my side. Everything had to work a certain way. Guys were swinging at bad pitches. I was getting borderline calls. The control was just there. I can't explain it. The control was just there. It pretty much came out of nowhere.

The first inning, I struck out the side and it didn't even cross my mind that I had good stuff, because I've struck out the side in the first inning, and gone and walked five or six in a row, and never gotten out of the second or third. Once I get into the fourth, it might sound a little goofy, but I loosen up even more in the fourth or fifth inning. Once I got through the fourth, I knew it was going to be a day where I could go out and just throw, and I didn't have to think about trying to hit corners and that. I just had that kind of stuff.

I was pumped in the ninth because it was the first time I had ever gone nine innings in my professional career. I knew I didn't have any walks. I knew I had a complete game with no walks and a bunch of strikeouts. I didn't know I was anywhere remotely close to 20. I thought maybe 16. I was excited about the complete game and no walks. I don't know when the next time will be when we'll see that for me.

Guys like Nolan Ryan and Roger Clemens and Randy Johnson and Curt Schilling, people come to watch that. Just like they come to watch Sammy and Mark hit home runs. Strikeouts and home runs. That's the two things in baseball that excites the fans. Sammy sells tickets. Strikeout pitchers sell tickets. You never know what's going to happen. You can go out and strike out 18, or 19, or even 20.

It's not hard to stay myself. Everybody knows I don't like to talk a lot or have a whole lot of attention. I guess when you win a Rookie of the Year Award or strike out 20, it's inevitable. I can handle it. I can do it. I just don't like it.

What would I be doing if I wasn't playing baseball? That's a pretty good question. I probably wouldn't be doing anything. I'd be living with my parents, they'd be supporting me. I wasn't big on school. I hated school. I've only got one talent. Fortunately, it worked for me. I've had success with it, and I'm going to ride it as long as I have it.

Kevin Orie

Kevin Orie was one of the top National League rookies in 1997, batting .275 in 114 games. Cub fans thought they'd finally found someone to succeed Ron Santo at third base. Heck, he'd lasted longer than Gary Scott (61 games). But Orie struggled in '98. He hit .140 in 50 games, was optioned to Class AAA Iowa on May 27, and traded to Florida two months later—but not before one memorable moment. On May 6, he just missed Ricky Gutierrez's single in the third inning. It was the only hit that day off Kerry Wood, who struck out a record-tying 20 Houston Astros.

I knew you were going to ask me about that. I remember it pretty well. It's just one of those strange plays. You make it almost every day all season. Everybody knows that defense was one of my strengths. It was just one of those balls hit to the left of me a little bit—a little more than a little bit. You never know—some balls are hit hard off the bat, and you try to get reads on how the grass affects it because the grass is pretty thick. The dirt, on the other hand, is pretty hard. I took an angle going after the ball. My first thought was that it was going to bounce. I don't know if it was a one-hopper, two-hopper. It looked like I could get there standing up. If I've got to dive, I dive. I won't dive to make a play look good. It was one of those in-betweeners. I thought I could stretch for it. The ball was there. It was strange. I saw it roll into the outfield. Plays like that happen. Going back, maybe if my first thought was to dive and smother it, I would've done that now. But sometimes you smother it and you may not get up cleanly or pick up the ball cleanly, and the guy still gets a hit.

It didn't even touch my glove. Unless it hit a string, I'm pretty sure it never touched anything. It's a play I make most of the time. It was one of those balls.

It was a fun game. It was easy. You were watching him go. He just dominated them. You never get to see that that often, and against Houston, too. As the game rolled on, by the seventh inning, guys started playing tighter. Gutierrez's hit was earlier on. The only thing I was getting tight about in the seventh was that I could see that it could haunt me. You start thinking, what's next?

I think a couple times I may have peeked back at left field and there were a group of "Ks." I was trying to count them. You take bits and pieces in throughout the game.

I'd never dreamt going into the season that things would turn out the way they did, that I'd be traded and out of a position by the end of May there. That was a very tough, very tough time for me. In a lot of ways, I still thought—or I still think—there's a chance I could still be playing over there today if the opportunity had been available longer and I'd had more time.

I came back from Iowa and that was it. My job was lost at that point, and I never got a chance to play after that. It was tough. I understand in a lot of ways how it works. But at the same time— being in the system for so long and coming through, and starting out there, and how things were supposed to be, and the little bit of support—I thought I'd be given an extra chance. You try to make changes and as soon as they don't start working out, that's what can happen.

I can honestly say I would've liked to have had a little more time there to work through it. Heck, it didn't have to be that year. Sacrifice the season and make it the next year. There's just not a lot of patience in baseball. It's not going to change. I've dealt with it and moved on, and it's sent me to a few different spots since then. You have a tendency to look back and say, "What if?"

I had such high expectations for that season. When I came back from Iowa, things were different, and I wasn't comfortable. I knew I wasn't going to be sitting there playing once a week, not at my age. At the time, maybe a change was fairly healthy for me. But at the same time, I really wasn't prepared to leave Chicago at that point. If I'd had a chance to control it, I would not have left.

You get all those years through the system. You get all the accolades, you're highly touted, and I made it through the first year all right. I had some tough luck with some of those wind balls. A month—you figure that wouldn't be enough to sign you off.

I was pretty close with all those guys. It was uncomfortable for them. They didn't know what to say to me. They didn't expect things to turn out the way they did for me. The pep talks were basically, "Do what you got to do, you'll be all right." It was just shocking to a lot of people. One 30-second phone call. "You're traded, things just didn't work out, here's your new GM. Be there by 4:00 P.M. for tomorrow's game." A lot of whirlwind. I was staring at my apartment full of stuff, like, what am I supposed to do? That was very weird.

I'm thankful I got to play there a little bit because I always wanted to. I used to go there from school. We'd sit in the bleachers. Whenever we had time to get away from baseball and school, we'd sneak up there to go to games.

Joe Girardi

A native of Peoria, Illinois, Joe Girardi grew up a Cub fan. He sat in the bleachers during his college days at Northwestern University. His dream to play for his childhood heroes came true when he was the Cubs' Opening Day catcher in 1989. He left involuntarily after the 1992 season when he was chosen by Colorado in the expansion draft. The move hurt, but Girardi also understood the business of baseball. "The hardest thing about changing teams is leaving your friends," he said. He would eventually play four seasons with the New York Yankees, winning three World Series rings. In 2000, Girardi rejected more money from two other teams to return home and rejoin the Cubs. Wife Kim and daughter Serena played a big part in his decision.

I remember sitting at home watching night games with my father on TV when the Cubs were on the road. I also remember traveling with my father in the summers—he was a salesman—and listening to Lou Boudreau and Jack Brickhouse do the games. There were four boys, and Dad used to take us up to the ballpark about 8 to 10 times a year. We'd drive up three hours. He always did it on a good giveaway. We always came on Bat Day and things like that and had a wonderful time.

I wrote a third-grade essay that I wanted to play for the Chicago Cubs. That was my dream. I have a lot of fond memories about coming to the ballpark. It's funny, what I remember the most about coming to the ballpark was the Ron Santo pizza. I used to get three or four pieces a game during the course of the game, and that's what I remember the most.

I would usually fall asleep in the chair next to my dad. We watched a lot of division rivals, Pittsburgh and the Phillies. I remember Mike Schmidt being a Cub killer. I was pretty amazed, Opening Day 1989, when I was actually on the same field that he was. That was like, pinch me and wake me up.

It's a lot different now because I'm a lot more mature and I don't think I'm necessarily taken aback by the surroundings and in awe like I was the first time I came here. The idea of coming to Wrigley Field and playing in this ballpark will never lose its appeal, even when I'm done playing and I bring my kids here.

Kim and I used to take the train down and sit in the bleachers. For us, it was a 20-minute ride on the train, get off behind the ballpark, and go sit in the bleachers. We did it a couple times. It was harder because at that time I was playing, and our season was going on, and we had practice every day. There was a two-week span between when our season was over and finals, and we'd take a day or two. I wasn't drafted yet, but Kim knew my dream was to play in the major leagues, and she told me she always believed I would make it.

Yankee Stadium, that's a special place. But it's different here because as a kid I didn't watch the Yankees, and I didn't grow up loving the Yankees. I grew up loving the Cubs. And to be able to fulfill your dreams is really special.

It was really important for me to come back to the Cubs for a number of reasons. I think the first reason was family. As you get older and have children, your priorities change. I wanted some stability for my family, and I wanted my daughter Serena to know her grandparents and her aunts and uncles like I did, because that was real important to me. I remember a lot of fond memories with family, aunts and uncles, grandparents, and I wanted Serena to know her grandparents. You're basically gone nine months out of the year.

Two, I got a chance to play for the team that I love playing for and I always wanted to play for. That was real important to me. I think last year—this might sound kind of funny—but last year was the first year I ever had to rent a U-Haul to come home. That's not easy to do.

Andy MacPhail

Andy MacPhail was named the Cubs president and chief executive offi-
cer in September 1994, after guiding the Minnesota Twins to two World
Series championships in 1987 and 1991 as general manager. He has been
unable to duplicate that success with the Cubs.

The only question I asked during my interview was if there were
any plans on the horizon to either leave Wrigley Field or do anything dramatically different, and the answer was no. That was
good enough for me because I don't want to be quarterbacking
that project.

The game has evolved. It's evolved beyond the game. It's entertainment now. The expectations of ownership have dramatically
changed. The allegiance of sports and its identification to the fans
has evolved. There are more sports, there is greater competition
for the athletes. They play other sports. We have expanded.

The expectations that your team will have a $10 million pay-
roll and go to the World Series and charge $12 for a box seat
behind the dugout at third base are unreal. Fans just feel that there
is an inalienable right. In fact, it's a game, and someone wins and
someone loses.

To me, any failures we have in the last five seasons have been more
at my doorstep than the Tribune Company's. I wish it was a
money issue. If I ever felt that money was keeping us from being
the difference in getting over the top, I think it would be the least
of our problems.

Our problems have been more getting the core type of players
to play good baseball over a consistent period of time. It has nothing to do with ownership and financial limitations. Some of those,
frankly, are self-imposed because I haven't decided to charge $50
for box seats, which others do. My job is to keep things as afford-

able and accessible as I can. The highest ticket price we sell is $25. There are 17 clubs who have higher-priced tickets than we do.

It's a natural thing for fans to want more. The franchise has struggled since '45 to get to the World Series. You've had different ownerships. But you've had more postseason appearances with the Tribune as owner than any other.

Yosh Kawano

He's at least as old as Wrigley Field's ivy. Yosh Kawano has been the Chicago Cubs' man behind the scenes since the 1940s. Officially, he has been the team's equipment manager since 1953 and was given emeritus status in 2000. Unofficially, he is the players' protector. You'll never get him to reveal any secrets about anybody—not even their shoe size. His uniform consists of a white floppy hat, baggy khaki pants, and a white t-shirt stained with tobacco and shoe polish. Yosh says he doesn't own anything with the Cubs' logo on it. He prefers to be anonymous.

I guess I grew up in ballparks. Wrigley Field in L.A. It was a huge, double-deck minor league park. I was the batboy, everything. The Cubs played a lot of games there because the Wrigleys owned it. Then they'd go to Catalina Island. You ever been to Catalina?

Gabby Hartnett. He was pretty friendly. Augie Galan. I got a letter from his wife the other day. He was a real good-looking guy. All the years he was here, he was single. He was really a ladies' man. They had to get an escort to get him out of the ballpark. On Ladies Day, they couldn't control themselves.

Gabby, he was a great big Irishman. He had a lot of relatives. You can't imagine how old we all are. We used to hang out at a place called Binyon's. That was my big hangout. Everybody knows me, all the politicians know me. Like the governor, he said, "Yoshie, you're always down at Binyon's all the time." Whenever these old-time ballplayers come in, they take them there. The old ladies, they see them and they go crazy. They say to the waiter, "That looks like Billy Torgenson or Augie Galan." I took Ted Lyons there one time. Ted Lyons, he was a really good-looking guy. Never married. You should have seen all the old ladies. I got a kick out of that Ted Lyons. He was a big star with the White Sox. Luke Appling. He came down there and met me down there.

We were in baseball when we were little kids. You don't know anything about the Depression, but in those days, kids didn't have

278

an automobile. You never thought about things like golf or things like that. You couldn't go to the beach because you had to have a car. Everybody thinks because you live in southern California you go to the beach. Heck, I could remember a lot of ballplayers who couldn't even swim. They never went.

I can't remember going to the beach. I was at the ballpark. You wouldn't believe the ballplayers in southern California on the south side when I was a kid. Ballplayers like Mickey Owen and Bobby Doerr. They were really good ballplayers, and they all lived in one area, and they were all poor. That was during the Depression, and it was really sad. You needed a job.

You know, a ballplayer, he can't do anything for himself. Once he puts on that uniform, somebody's got to do things for him. It's not that they're lazy. They can't go out to get a hot dog, or they can't go to the office, or something like that. No, man. "Yosh, did you get that morning paper? Would you get me one?" They can't go out here and get one. I had a ballplayer one time had a motor-cycle, he went back out here and went to the parking lot and was going down the street. Somebody told me they were looking for him and I said he was taking a ride. Joe Wallis. I think Pepitone did that, too. They weren't in their complete uniform, but they had their uniform pants on and a t-shirt, and off they went.

Sandberg and I, we're pretty close. I think—you hate to say this word—but he trusted me. A lot of these players, they don't know who to trust. You get these people, these PR people. These players got to believe they're getting used a little bit. I don't think I introduced Sandberg to four or five people in my life. I know he was uncomfortable with that.

Ever been to Gibson's? It's a real nice restaurant. It's kind of an "in" place. I'm not much for steaks, but it's a great place for all the celebrities. It's a known fact that Sid Luckman was the owner there. Well, Sid's my friend. We've been friends since I first started around the ballpark. Gee, he's a nice guy. The best. Steve Lombardo, one of the managing partners there, he knows that Sid and

I are good friends. We were in the restaurant, Sandberg and his wife and me and Arlene were there. I still hadn't introduced Sandberg to him. We were waiting for the car and I said, "Steve, this is my friend, Ryne Sandberg." It's not rude on my part, but that's the way it is. These guys—you ever introduce any of these guys to anybody? Who cares? They mean a lot to me.

Ah, Dawson. What can you say about a guy like that? A perfect guy. He's everything. So patient. It seemed like he always has time for you. Ever see him walking down the concourse here? He always stops. He doesn't say anything, but he looks and he kind of smiles and he laughs. One day, we were in a clubhouse and all the batboys were just standing there, and he's sitting on the table and they're telling them stories, and he's just laughing. I was watching from the side. I don't know how long he was there. They did all the talking. Every one of those kids. How many times do you see that? It's like he was interested in what each one had to say. He'd laugh. I got a kick out of that. Ain't that nice? That's something that today, very few people have—time. They can't give up any time.

I don't know how much longer. I don't know any other life. I'll tell you what. I never thought I'd be here this long.

INDEX